WHEN SPACE MEETS ART

Spatial, Structural and Graphic Design
for Event and Exhibition

CONTENT

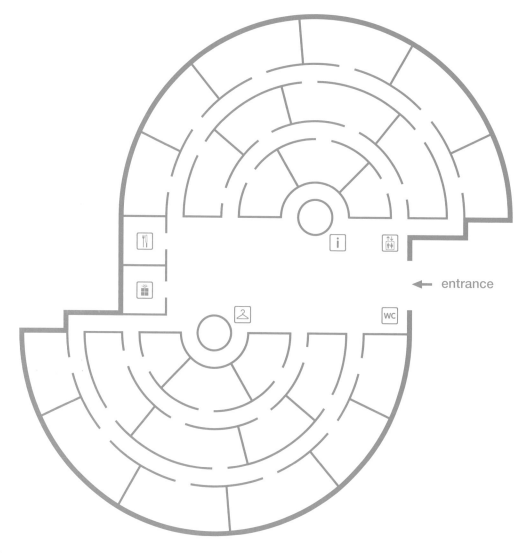

← entrance

INTRO

WHEN SPACE MEETS ART

Designing an event is quite a task. It is an act of storytelling, bringing abstract concept like 'establishing positive image of new launched products in trade shows' to concrete event design that you can enjoy and perceive the ultimate messages, be it through contemplation or experience.

From the brief of event objectives to concept generation, event design involves the actualization of intangible ideas to realistic experiences - to let visitors step into it and perceive the messages behind through the entire event experiences with integration of internal factors such as installation, interior decoration, audio, performers, as well as mechanical and computer interactive; and external factors like promotional flyers, posters, invitations and advertising. All these elements contributed in events are necessary to be 'meaningful' and 'fascinating' from the audiences' point of view in terms of attraction. In an event, different fields of design act together in a set. It is a spatial and graphic bombardment to give a real-life experience impressing not only the first row, but also the entire community who takes part in.

Event is a spatial experience where we put on the air what exactly we want to say by assorted building blocks in one fell swoop. Can you recall any experience in recent events? Do you remember what the designers wanted to say? Or did you just concentrate on individual exhibited objects, and play the interactive games around without understanding the main theme? Luminous events require deliberating arrangement of all parts in space, both fixed and in motion, in order to create a powerful and memorable relationship between visitors and the exhibition's content. All elements contributing in the events have to be unified with the main theme, giving the same idea and eventually complete the whole story. An event is a living, three-dimensional symphony to be experienced and engaged, bringing messages, brands, and business direction to life. A triumphant event is always presented with a superb communication approach. It can make everyone remembers what it tells. It is the journey that is possible to change your intrinsic value and expectation towards events, like you will probably aware of the social problem in children abuse if the events bring you to the gloomy world of abused children.

What's more, event has to be executional by incorporating all parts efficiently and effectively. It involves the amalgamation of designers' deliberation, logistics, installation, sound, speeches, public promotion etc. so as to transform abstract ideas to concrete design. Designers play the most important role; their design needs to be communicative, impactful and executive. MET Studio Design demonstrated an incredible work on it. You will probably become a specialist in environmental issues if you have been to the Hong Kong Wetland Park designed by the talents. MET Studio Design created an interactive tour, showing the wetland habitat in one of the world busiest cities. You will enter the Visitor Centre in the semi-submerged location below the ground level at the approach side beneath a grass canopy roof; and alongside go into a real peat swamp featuring live crocodiles. The delightful design with integration of natural and scientific approaches makes the eco-park one of the most important tourist destinations in the town, as well as contributes significantly to the local economy.

While most modern events give interactive voyage, some events are intended to encourage contemplation and stimulate creativity. You will probably be excited with the exploration of the new use of fibers by Tokujin Yoshioka in Tokujin Yoshioka × Lexus L-finesse-Evolving Fiber Technology 2006. Have you ever come across the special artifacts with only fibers, or shapeless fiber particles? Every event is an inspiration; through the bombardments of spatial elements with art, there are always new horizons for you to explore.

All events, despite of topic, share the intrinsic tension between the aims of the host and the experiences of the viewer, having an active role or not. 'When Space Meets Art' graces the pages with the assimilation of space, structure and graphics that makes event surprising and turns into remarkable fascination. The entire area is the biggest yet impacful entity to create most attention to audience. Designers are bringing their inspiration in front of your eyes from raw rocks to fine stage of aspiration. Work from international artists like Bruce Mau Design Inc., Karim Rashid Inc. and WATdesign will be demonstrated to bring you the impact of how spatial essentials affect your impression in event experiences. Turn the book at your best handiness and experience the impact of how space collides with art elements in event installation and executions. We are going to reveal different event designs all over the world. Ready yet? Get set and go to the Laputa of Events!

Krizia Moving Shapes

by Migliore+Servetto Architetti Associati

Client: Krizia
Art Direction: Ico Migliore (Graphics), Mara Servetto
Design: Migliore+Servetto Architetti Associati
Photography: Studio M2, Tokyo
Year: 2001

Exhibition design created for a big retrospective exhibition on Krizia organized at the Museum of Contemporary Art of Tokyo – MOT, Tokyo, Japan – The design is conceived as a circular itinerary that passes through the different theme areas of the exhibition, which are characterized by a different setting. The exhibition design is filled with large and simple displays that animate the museum space. The large spaces underscore the dynamic of the design, which is no longer experienced as a static entity, but as a moving spectacle. This was created with the help of the right lighting and motorised technical elements.

The first exhibition area contains a large wall devoted to knitwear. This is followed by a rectangular room where six tall structural steel portals, regularly placed at the centre, containing six groups of fashions arranged in themes and suspended above floor level.

The gallery leads to the main room where large suspended volumes move upwards and downwards progressively revealing seven different families of clothing. In the last area, dynamic graphics are projected upon a large screen made of white knitwear.

Juxtaposing the projection are eight suspended polycarbonate sheets covered by a specially polarized film that allows the clothing to be viewed only from certain points. In this way, fashions are alternately revealed and concealed to the passing visitor.

ROMANTICISM IS
A LONG STRING
OF PEARLS.
ROMANTICISM IS
A LONG STRING
OF PEARLS.
ROMANTICISM IS
A LONG STRING
OF PEARLS.
ROMANTICISM IS
A LONG STRING
OF PEARLS.

Guggenheim Museo,
di Tatlin,

acielo Chrysler.

moscho.

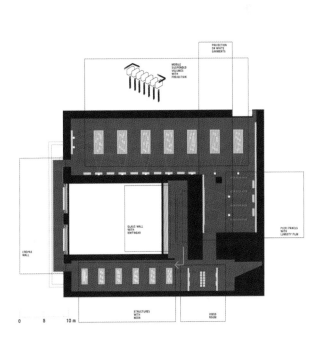

Wallpaper* Urban Addition
by Migliore+Servetto Architetti Associati

Client: Wallpaper Magazine UK*
Art Direction: Ico Migliore, Mara Servetto
Design: Migliore+Servetto Architetti Associati
Photography: Donato Di Bello
Year: 2001

Communicate Wallpaper* magazine leadership as trend setter by creating partnership events with top level companies that present cutting-edge design products and concepts – This exhibition design project deals with urban addition and evocates an urban domestic lifestyle. Space is cancelled out with dark floor or carpet and there is no environmental lighting. Illumination is only focused on the products or displays.

Design is articulated in three spaces: external access corridor, main place of modular display sets and prefabricated house.

In the main place there are eleven openings in the floor, fitted with inclined mirrors that illuminate and subdivide the space. Inside this area, there is a ten-metre high, prefabricated house designed by the architect Oscar Kaufmann: on the outside backlit screen prints reproduce stylized facades.

The whole exhibition design presents a mix use of light, multimedia video projection, and graphic signs. In addition, there are right and reflected fluorescent lights and synchronized dynamic projections that flow over two screens of 13 x 10 metres.

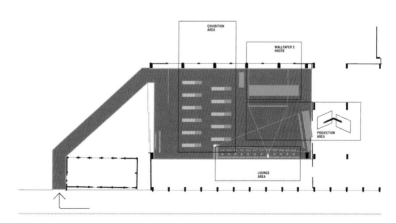

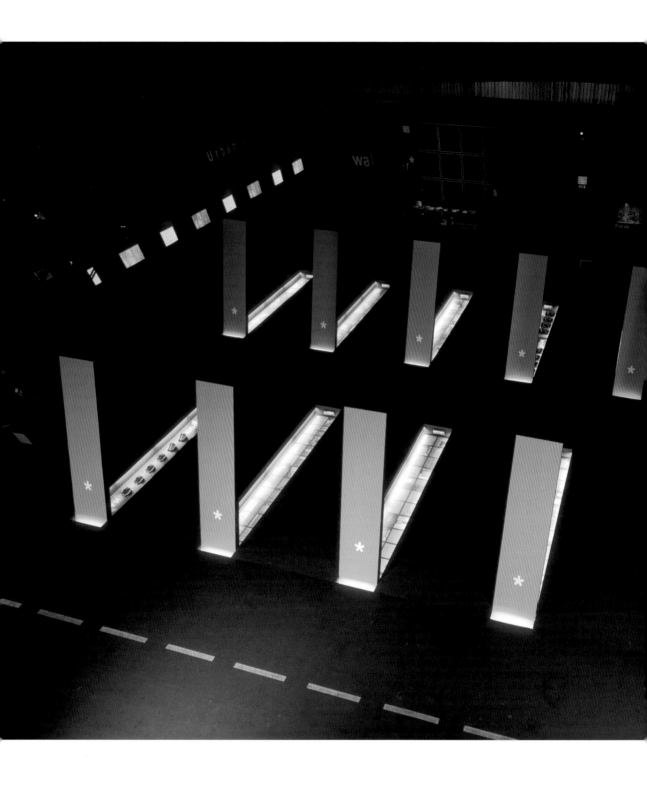

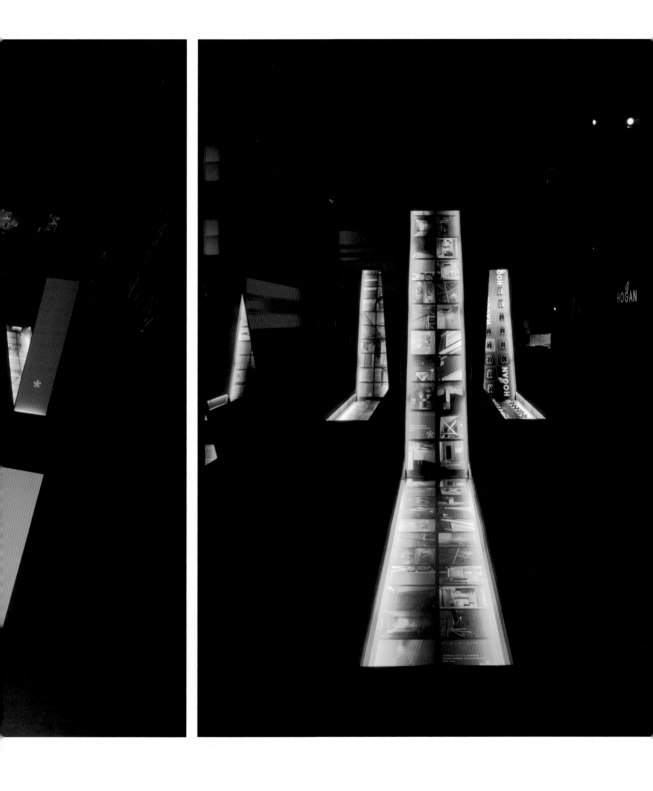

Client: Boffi
Art Direction: Ico Migliore, Mara Servetto
Design: Migliore+Servetto Architetti Associati
Photography: Duilio Bitetto
Year: 2003

Exhibition design created for the opening of Boffi's Milan showroom – For the opening of Boffi's Milan showroom, the firm's history is recounted by a dynamic installation that uses 200 metres of ribbon images and graphics. Hung from the ceiling, they run across a flexible transparent support and are overlaid with as many metres of variable-field electroluminiscent lighting which switches on with programmed dissolves.

The interpretation of superimposed images unfolds continously, supplemented by synchronised animations projected onto three transparent holographic screens suspended among the ribbons.

On the floor above, the story is run horizontally through a sequence of rooms and allows for a closer reading of the images. In the external courtyard graphic animations are projected on a screen of 6 x 6 metres welcoming visitors.

New Wave

by Migliore+Servetto Architetti Associati

Client: Wallpaper* Magazine UK
Art Direction: Ico Migliore, Mara Servetto
Design: Migliore+Servetto Architetti Associati
Photography: Donato Di Bello
Year: 2003

Communicate Wallpaper* magazine's leadership as trend setter by creating partnership events with top level companies that present cutting-edge design products and concepts – The exhibition design shows a wood and tensed fabric real scale reconstruction of the Wallypower 118 boat on the right side of the internal space. It is a scenic and dynamic representation aiming at evocating a modern lifestyle and hightech boat characteristics, through the projection of huge scale movies and multimedia devices.

The virtual model of the boat is set against the material presence of specific Wally lifestyle products and elements. On the other side of the boat there is in fact a 30 metres platform positioned at different heights, that includes lifestyle products and boat elements. The platform is marked with lines of light created by electroluminescent lightings. Video projections as well as graphic signs and images appear as displayed objects.

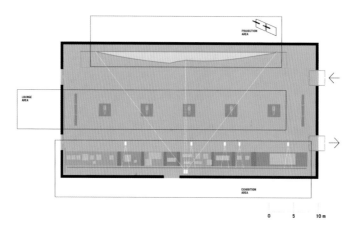

Habitar el món
by Base

Client: Forum 2004
Art Direction/Design: Base
Year: 2004

For this convention in Barcelona, organized to address world issues, Base was invited to develop the identity for one of the four main exhibitions being held on the Forum site, 'Habitar el món' ('Inhabiting the world'). The themes presented in the exhibition – pollution, poverty, hunger, disease – were broken down to three levels: world, city, people. The exhibition started with largest, world view and progressed to a personal level to show what people can do to make a difference. Base's LAB division created a program for the event that translates any image to round pixels, a reference to the world issues at hand. With a matching dot matrix typeface, messages and images could be applied at any size – from the exhibition catalog to huge exterior supergraphics. Base's contributions include the exhibition's installations and graphics, creative direction of the audiovisuals, and the catalog published for the event.

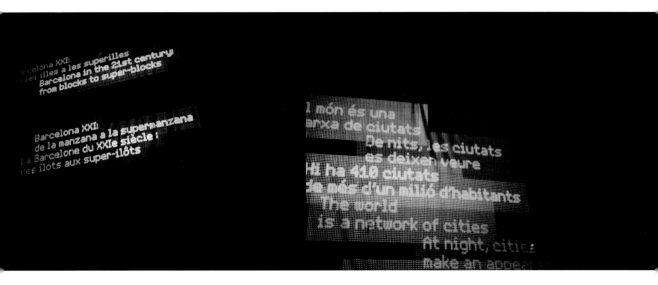

Barcelona XXI:
de les illes a les superilles
Barcelona in the 21st century:
from blocks to super-blocks

Barcelona XXI:
de la manzana a la supermanzana
La Barcelone du XXIe siècle :
des îlots aux super-îlots

El món és una
xarxa de ciutats
De nits, les ciutats
es deixen veure
Al he 410 ciutats
de més d'un milió d'habitants
The world
is a network of cities
At night, cities
make an appearance

Habitar el Món

Wer
Should
use
uclear

nations want
and we're going to
have to get it from
somewhere

Sparking Reaction at Sellafield Visitors' Centre

by Nick Bell Design

Client: Science Museum, London UK
Art Direction/Design: Nick Bell
Year: 2001-02

It was an exhibition for the Science Museum at British Nuclear Fuel's visitors centre at Sellafield. With the proviso of having full editorial control, the Museum agreed to the commission from BNFL to improve the public image of the visitor centre – which was perceived by many as an apologia for the nuclear industry.

At the heart of the exhibition concept was the desire for people to engage with written text. The Core, an immersive space both physically and intellectually at the centre of the exhibition within which large-scale animated text and images were projected onto the floor and containing walls,

was the result. It was an intriguing and thought-provoking introduction to the debate about how Britain is powered. Motion was used with the clear-sighted purpose of making the hundreds of varied opinions in the sequence attractive to read. The idea was that people should be shocked or at least disquieted, by the facts and opinions on show – with the hope of provoke them into participating in the debate and having their say.

Exhibition John Maeda:
Nature + Eye'm Hungry

by Mathieu Lehanneur

Client: Fondation Cartier, Paris
Art Direction: Mathieu Lehanneur with
the collaboration of John Maeda
Design: Mathieu Lehanneur
Year: 2006

Mathieu Lehanneur was assigned to create a live reactive stage design by using motorized censored benches. In the projection room, seven benches slowly move in all directions. When a bench comes into contact with a wall or a visitor, it immediately goes off in the opposite direction. As soon as a visitor sits down, the bench stops. The designer is also required to give the perspective of an animated space by a computer program. He created a 'spatio-temporal loophole' between the projection room and the interaction room. In fact, a transitional corridor between these two spaces gives the visitor the sensation that he is shrinking and that he is leaving the real world (change of scale, sound absorption, reducing lighting).

Materials: Alveolar sandwich panels, Motorized mobile benches, PVC canvas, Steel structure, Video projectors.

Le Futur, a-t-il un avenir?

by Base

Client: Le Pass
Art Direction/Design: Base
Year: 2000

'Le Futur, a-t-il un avenir?' means 'The Future, Does It Have a Future?.' Having designed in 2000 the visual identity and launch campaign for this 'science adventure park,' Base was brought on to design the visuals and signage for its exhibition about sustainable development. Using furniture and architecture as primary vehicles for thematic support, the studio applied a wood-textured stencil typeface and incorporated recycled computer keyboards and monitors into a series of interactive learning stations. The Palais des Images – Le Pass's state-of-the-art movie theater – features projections on three walls and the floor and ceiling for an experience that surrounds visitors and makes them feel involved in the theme. Supergraphics on the building exterior were composed of a massive grid of square pixels that presented the exhibition title and a series of pictograms that would communicate with the park's multilingual visitors.

The Good Life: New Public Spaces for Recreation

by Project Projects

Client: The Van Alen Institute
Art Direction: Prem Krishnamurthy, Adam Michaels
Design: Caroline Askew, Chris McCaddon, Ken Meier, Justin Smith
Photography: Elizabeth Felicella
Year: 2006

The Good Life: New Public Spaces for Recreation was a large-scale exhibition featuring 70 international design projects for urban public space. The exhibition transformed an empty building at the end of Pier 40 on the West Side of Manhattan into a fun destination for the general public. The exhibition design (a collaboration with architects Work AC) consisted of a single snaking sheet of yellow fabric, hung from the ceiling, which incorporated strips of printed vinyl and video screens.

Project Projects designed the identity, printed materials, website, exhibition graphics, and motion graphics for the exhibition. The overall exhibition identity is a simple, optimistic yellow circle containing the logotype. The logo was represented

physically by the balloon with diameter of 10 feet which floated above the exhibition venue; this created interest and also functioned as a wayfinding tool. The show's contents were divided into five themed sections; each was treated with a distinctive pattern and colour scheme. Materials presenting each project - texts, still images, videos, interviews - were displayed through combination of printed vinyl sheets and twenty individual video loops.

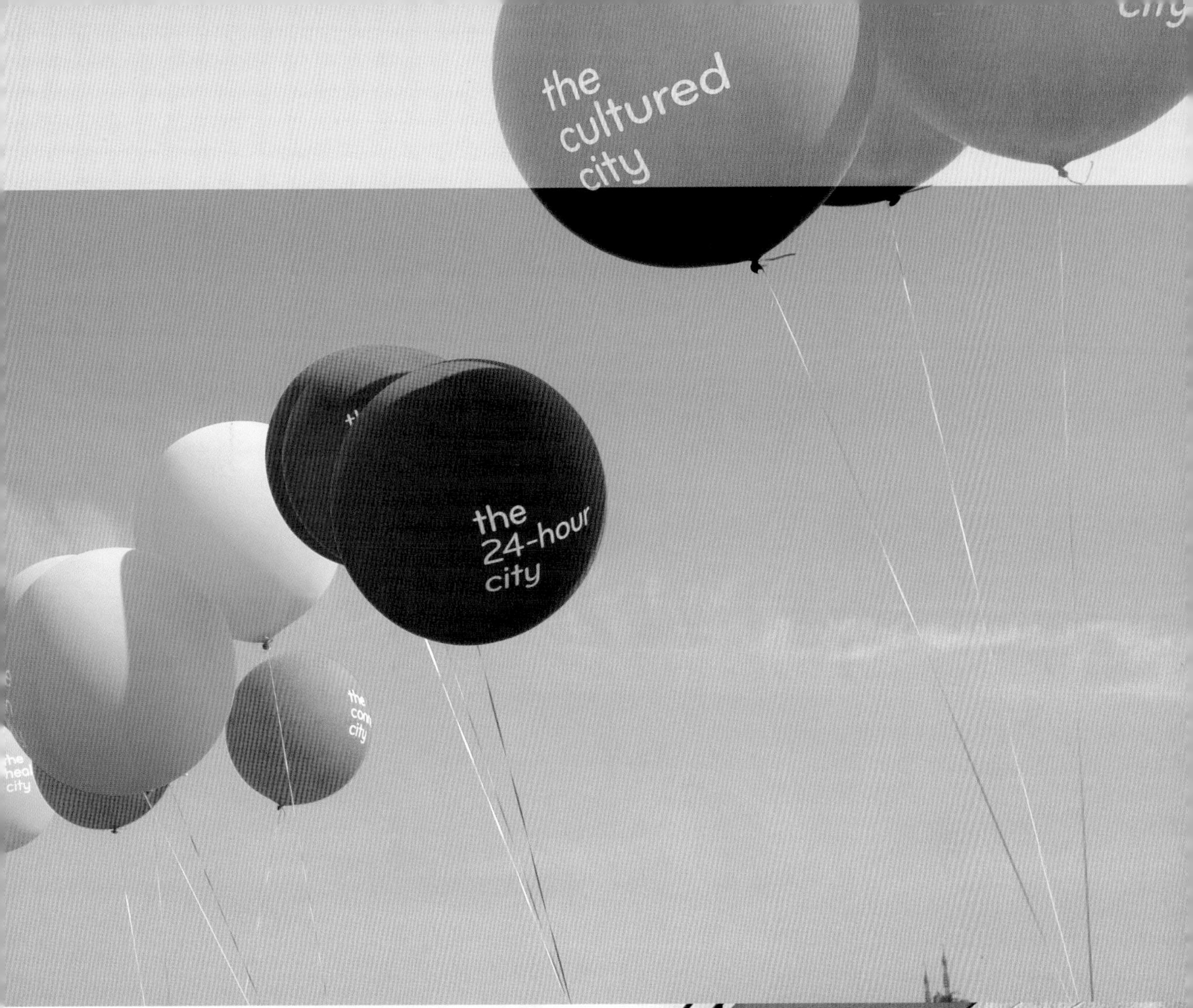
the cultured city
the 24-hour city

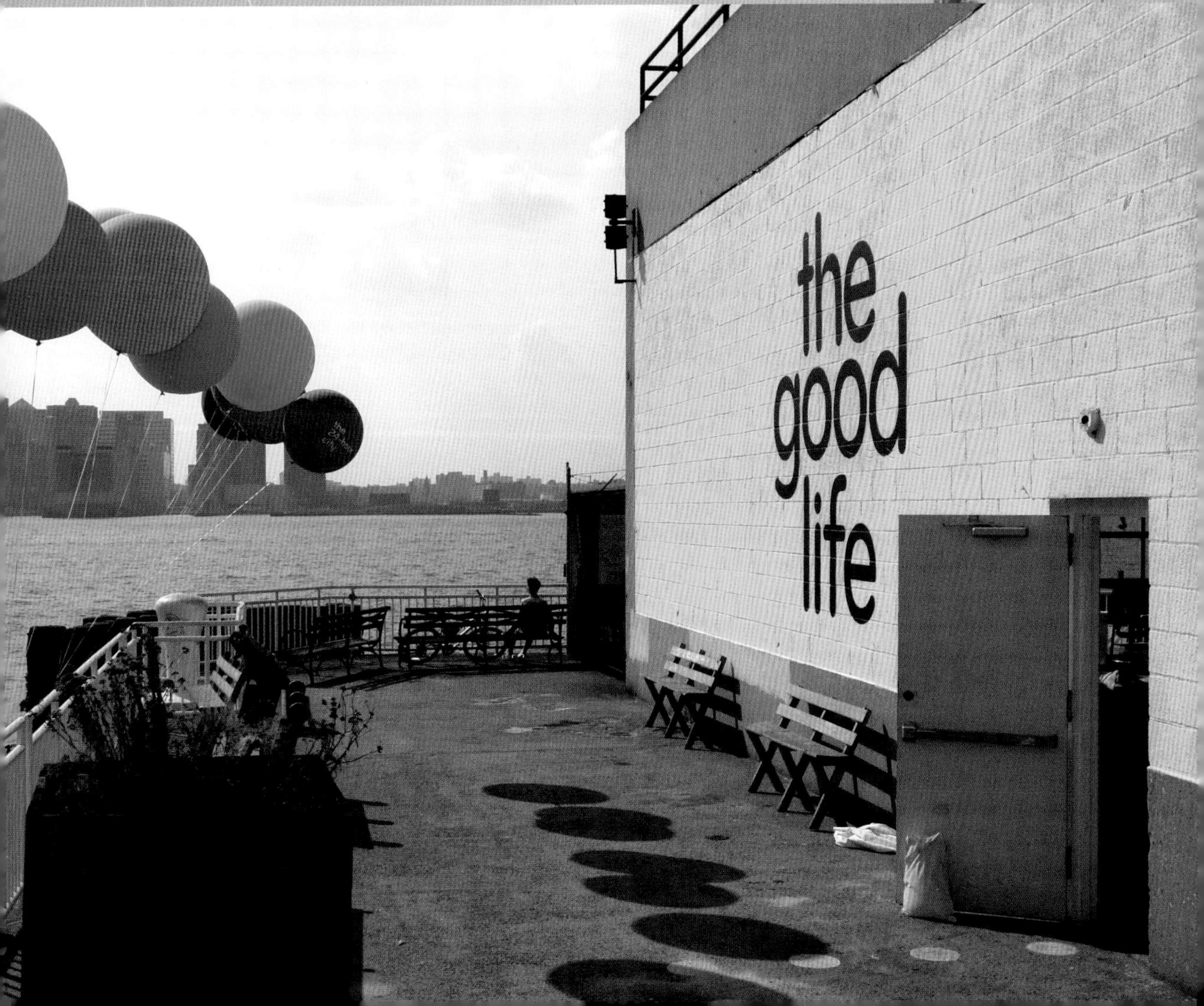
the good life

NorthSouthEastWest – A 360° View of Climate Change

by Browns

Client: The Climate Group in partnership with British Council
Art Direction: Nick Jones
Design: Chris Wilson
Year: 2005

It is an exhibition to illustrate not just the causes and impacts of global climate changes but also highlight the solutions being implemented to reduce greenhouse gas emissions worldwide. There is also an accompanying book.

The solution is worldwide touring exhibition that focuses on 10 climate issues in 12 locations featuring 10 Magnum photographers and 10 contributors as diverse as Tony Blair and Leonardo DiCaprio. The exhibition is a modular 'tile' based system that 'hangs' around an aluminium frame and can be presented in almost any size and configuration required. The smallest to date uses 48 tiles, the largest 132. The standard configuration is a tower, 1 metre square and 2 metres tall. Browns worked with Standard 8 to develop and manufacture the system.

The project has been wonderfully received with a number of organizations approaching The Climate Group as a result. The exhibition was exhibited in the Science Museum in London and has so far visited Melbourne, Adelaide, Sydney, Oslo, San Francisco, Brussels, Japan, New York and many more. The project was undertaken in partnership with the British Council.

All paper used and the printers were FSC accredited and the greenhouse gas emissions associated with the book are being offset via certified gold standard projects.

Massive Change
by Bruce Mau Design Inc.

Client: Vancouver Art Gallery
Art Direction: Bruce Mau
Design: Studio project
Year: 2002 - Present

Since 2002, Bruce Mau Design has been working on communicating, through different media, a set of ideas about the future of global design. BMD believes that design has emerged as one of the world's most powerful forces. It has placed us at the beginning of a new, unprecedented period of human possibility, where all economies and ecologies are becoming global, relational, and interconnected. In order to understand these emerging forces, there is an urgent need to articulate precisely what we are doing to ourselves and to our world. This is the ambition of Massive Change. So far, Massive Change exists as an international exhibition, a book, public events, a communication campaign, a radio program and a line of products.

The Massive Change exhibition, commissioned by the Vancouver Art Gallery, opened there on October 2, 2004. An exploration and map of design's new capacity, power, and promise, the exhibition opened at the Art Gallery of Ontario in Toronto on March 11th 2005. It will subsequently travel to the Museum of Contemporary Art in Chicago in September 2006, and on to Europe and Asia. In conjunction with the exhibition, the Vancouver Art Gallery presented an international speakers' event called 'Massive Change Visionaries' that tapped into the ideas and innovations of today's leading thinkers and producers. Each Massive Change venue will have a unique series of pubic events – lectures, symposia, and workshops – exploring the questions raised in the project.

'Massive Change,' the book, published internationally by Phaidon Press, explores our new design potential and celebrates our global capacities – while casting a cautious look at our limitations.

Massive Change radio, originally broadcast on CIUT 89.5 FM in Toronto during 2003, is archived on the comprehensive Massive Change website, www.massivechange.com. Each hour-long radio show offers live interviews with provocative thinkers across disciplines.

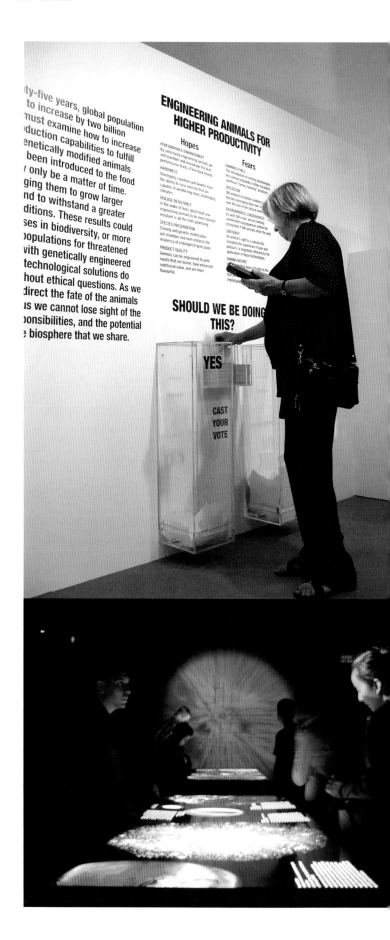

Future Force Warrior

Sticky Situation

Hydrate or Die

Natick Soldiers

Natick Soldier Systems Center is designing the soldier of the future. A division of the U.S. Army Soldier Systems Center (SSC), Natick is supervising a seven-year, US$250 million project called Future Force Warrior (FFW). Part of the Department of Defense's Future Combat Systems, it will begin testing in 2008.

The SSC is a DoD installation responsible for "the technology development and engineering, fielding, and sustainment of our military's food, clothing, shelters, airdrop systems, and soldier support."

Krazy Glue

Camelbak

At the Hotter 'n Hell Hundred bicycle race in Texas, temperatures can soar above 100° F, water stops are up to three hours apart, and reaching for a water bottle mounted on the bike frame is potentially dangerous. Preparing for his first race, Michael Eidson drew from his past experience as a paramedic. Eidson attached medical tubing to an I.V. bag, stuffed the bag into a sock, and sewed it onto the back of a t-shirt. One ride with the contraption convinced him to commercialize the which he dubbed the Camelbak.

In a clear example of adoption of Army

Wealthy
in Mobility

657
International passenger arrivals
worldwide each year, in millions

104
Bicycles produced worldwide,
in 2002, in millions

41
Cars produced worldwide,
in 2002, in millions

**Change Maker: Institute
for Transportation
and Development Policy**

Wealthy
in Measures to
End Suffering

1000
Children immunized against polio
to date, worldwide, in millions

30
Landmines destroyed since the
International Campaign to Ban Landmines
began in 1992, in millions

3
Antiretroviral treatments for
given to HIV/AIDS sufferers by the
World Health Organization by 2005,
in millions

**Change Maker:
Pledge 25 Club**

Wealthy
in Choices

35

6.7

33

27

2.7

18.8

2.9

100

33

**Wealthy
in Shared
Information**

100
Images produced worldwide
each year, in billions

73
Google searches each year, in billions

85
Viewers made aware of human rights issues, through
targeted presentations by Witness, an NGO that puts
cameras in the hands of local activists, in millions

5.8
Logos, labels and ads seen
by the average American
each year, in millions

**Change Makers:
The People of the
Philippines**

**Wealthy
in Sheer Capit**

27
Global annual GDP, in trillions of U.S. dollars

16
Uncounted, unpaid volunteer hours in a year,
what revolutionary economist Jeremy Rifkin
calls the "caring economy," in billions

9.3
Total value of "dead capital"—real estate
illegally owned by the world's poor, as one
economist, Hernando De Soto, in trillions of

6
Value of U.S. mutual funds, in trillions of

**Change Makers:
Grameen Bank**

What Makes You Wealthy
by Bruce Mau Design Inc.

Client: Bruce Mau Design Inc.
Art Direction: Bruce Mau
Design: Studio project
Year: 2004

The project is an annual 3-day design exposition featuring manufacturers, distributors, retailers and designers exhibiting product and services in addition to design exhibitions and a speaker's forum. BMD was commissioned to design an exhibit around the theme 'What Makes You Wealthy?'

Bruce Mau on wealth:
I'm sick of modern design.
I'm fed up with corporate cool.
I can't stand 'interior design.'
I hate those designer guys – I love 'em – but I detest that fabricated, artificial, managed, art-directed look.
I can't bear to see one more 'continuous surface.'

I've had it with perfection.
I hate the clean lines.
No more computer aided design.
Down with colour consultants.
Down with advertising. Down with PR.
Turn off TV.
Down with minimalism – we want maximalism.
Down with reduction – we want more! more! more!
Wealth?
Wealth is time.
Wealth is children.
Wealth is love.
Wealth is ideas, invention, exploration.
Wealth is books.
Wealth is collaboration, colleagues, friends, working together.
We're sick of the fake and phony.
We want it real.
Forget bandwidth.
We don't need a get-away, we need a get-to.

Ideal House

by Karim Rashid Inc.

Client: Cologne Fair
Art Direction/Design: Karim Rashid
Year: 2003

The world is becoming very visually savvy and info-savvy. The energy and times are hypertrophic. Consumers are perpetually interested in being stimulated, in being excited about their physical environment. It is the residue of the digital age. If the virtual world is so flexible, so personalized so complex, and so aesthetic, why not the physical world?

The technorganic house is the INFORMA-TION HOUSE. A flexible wired connected seamless interface house. Perfect design /formal design/good taste/classicism/ minimalism all these notions are over. Rashid sees the world's new domestic environment becoming more technological, more engaging, and softer – a Sensualism (minimalism and digital aesthetics through metapho the infostethicr). Soft is not just relegated to form and shape but also refers to new material landscape where tactile surfaces give people comfortable engaging physical experiences. Polymers, such as synthetic rubbers, silicones, transparencies, l.c.d. polymer wallpapers, all

contribute to this new softness of interior environment. The designer has heightened our experiences via touch. Materials in our spaces can now flex, change, morph, shift colour, cool and heat, etc. due to the Smart material movement. Smart materials are materials that communicate and give us feedback. New stimulating phenomena all play a role in our new 'relaxed' environments. Our spaces need to be free, free of history, free of tradition, flexible and customizable.

If freedom were a form it would be a never-ending undulating boundless biomorphic shape that is in perpetual motion. Form follows Fluid. In a post-industrial house – the information house our conditions will be more relaxed, less rigid, soft not hard, where our experiences will be more hypertextual and less linear. It is not a coincidence that the driving force behind the changing and ever-shifting global lifestyles is becoming more casual, more relaxed, softer, blobular, if you will.

More conceptually, the designer developed an installation for a 1994 exhibition in Tokyo entitled 'The Personal Digital Environment.' The space was 'wired' through the floor with a grid of low-voltage current and data transfer capabilities, providing instantaneous tele-audio-sensorial communications. The furniture and walls were connected to the wiring, rendering them 'live.' The idea is that, through the manipulation of touch screen or audio or brain-wave feedback, the occupant can change the environment instantaneously, altering qualities such as light, heat, smell, and humidity. By touching the pellucid surfaces, images, text, and sound can be surfed, scanned, changed, and morphed. In effect, the room acquires a life, becoming the interface for direct or indirect relations with strangers, data, and imagery, and crosses the bounds of history, fiction and reality, time and space.

These are the ideas around the Ideal house. The 'style' is infostethic – where the forms, spaces, shapes, colours all speak about our digital age.

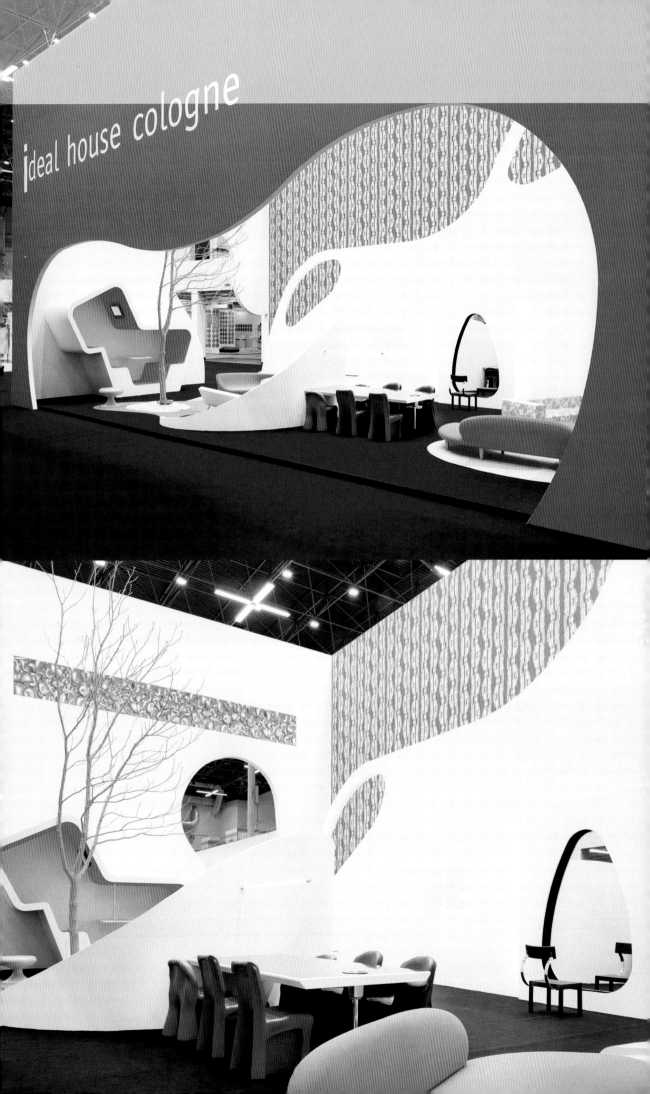

ideal house cologne

Kit 24 House
by Karim Rashid Inc.

Client: Interior Design Show
Art Direction/Design: Karim Rashid
Year: 2006

In February 2006, prolific designer Karim Rashid will unveil a concept space created especially for the eighth annual Interior Design Show. The installation, sponsored by The Globe and Mail, is named Kit 24 and is inspired by Rashid's interest in the notion of housing that can be erected simply and quickly, and is both inexpensive and democratic. Kit 24 is a house produced with simple, minimal parts and tooling. Rashid's environment is composed of a few repeated parts that assemble a 24-sided house, but it is also a metaphor for time and is based on a 24-hour day.

'I have always loved the idea of a Kit house,' says Rashid. The concept has been approached by engineers and architects throughout the years. The designer wanted to show the contemporary approach, a really positive, interesting and artistic space for living inspired by technology. It also provides a venue to show many of the designer's furnishings and objects; although all quite different from each other, they can cohabitate a space to communicate an organic, pleasurable environment.

Client: Hong Kong Heritage Museum
Page 52-55: Tommy Li Design Workship Limited
Art Direction: Thomas Siu
Design: Joshua Lau
Year: 2006

'MEGartSTORE' is an alternative exhibition experience, attempting to present contemporary artworks with an unusual and experimental approach. The exhibition is conceived to explore different ways of defining, appreciating and presenting art. In the past, museum was a sacred altar for the display of art and history; an opulent palace for the demonstration of wealth and power. However, it was during the modernization of museum in the later part of the 20th century that people began to rethink the role of museum in our contemporary society. As a result, new functions for museum and new concepts for exhibition evolved, linking art and history closer to our way of thinking and our way of living.

'MEGartSTORE' is taken from the word 'mega-store/mega-mall.' Tommy Li Design Workshop Limited, who was responsible for the identity/branding of the event, names this exhibition as 'MEGartSTORE' with the purpose of displaying and mixing more than 300 pieces of museum art collections in various subject matters and creative media under one roof in order to initiate new ways of seeing, appreciating and thus new meanings to the artworks.

The designer also wants to challenge visitors by suggesting a fun way of looking at art, and to serve as a catalyst to aestheticize the shopping experiences of our daily lives. Reminded that 'Shopping' is the most popular daily habits for Asian, average 2.5 times per week.

Page 56-59: Meta4 Design Forum Ltd
Art Direction/Design: Steven Chu, Anson Tsang,
Kenneth Tse, Humphrey Wong
Year: 2006

Held at the Hong Kong Heritage Museum from 4 June 2006 to 27 November 2006, 'MEGartSTORE', same as the previous project, attempts to investigate the ever blurring distinction between merchandise and (mass-)art in the rising world of materialism. While merchandises are being re-packaged as artworks of connoisseurs' interest and rarity; (real) art, on the other hand, remains a territory explored only by the few who look beyond the veil of this materialistic society. The curators of the exhibition turn this phenomenon upside-down and re-package artworks into (pseudo-)merchandise, thus luring everyday consumers into the world of art and self-exploration. The exhibition is shaped in an uncanny yet familiar setting: a shopping expedition to various stores.

Asia is facing an unprecedented identity crisis: while its economic outlook is as promising as an as-yet undiscovered New World, its cultural heritage seems like getting diluted as fast as its exponential growth factor. This exhibition is not an attempt to investigate into the east-west clash; however, it explores the underlying and the more fundamental issue of global unification: indistinction. In an attempt to bring out this dilemma in a casual yet pin-pointing gesture, the exhibition uses various means and concepts to guide visitors into a world of its own: enjoying the uncertainty of its identity. Through the techniques of spatial and lighting manipulation with selective mimicry, Meta4

Design Forum Ltd, who was responsible for the interior of the exhibition, pushed the visitors into a state of self-reflectance of their whereabouts. While sometimes we do enjoy a fleeting moment of uncertainty, however, we should always be fully conscious of the cause of that uncertainty.

Previous page left: Home & Garden
The 'Home-Art-Labyrinth-Store' is
a distorted furniture store where
artworks of various media, instead of
furniture items, are showcased. This
special setting provides the audience
with a new space for imagination and
a different perspective of appreciation.

Previous page right: Food & Beverage
The food packaging is so appealing
that your heart drools even more.
However, underneath the colourful
packaging is only an indistinctive
item. The trends of globalization have
stripped away every individual trait,
leaving behind a product with no
personalities or depth.

This page: Leisure & Entertainment
When the purchase is done and the
goods are consumed, the blistering
pack silently leaves a footprint of its
content, starting to disclose to us its
true materiality. If you take a reversed
view from the packing, you'll realize it
re-captures the dances of light, colour
and silhouette, giving us the most
psychedelic way to see the world.

Next page: Health & Beauty
A fashion boutique is used as a medium
to present the artworks. Some works
are 're-displayed' in a way that you
can only catch a glimpse of them, so
as to convey the message that external
beauty will be gone in a blink.

Expo 2000

by Marcel Wanders Studio

Client: World Expo 2000, Hanover
Art Direction/Design: Marcel Wanders
Photogrpahy: Daniël Nicolas (Royal Wing Room),
Maarten van Houten (VIP-chair)
Year: 2000

The Royal Wing Room is the heart of the little green island floating on top of the remarkable Dutch Pavilion. Designed by the Dutch Designer Marcel Wanders and his studio the elliptical room makes you feel like you're stepping into a different world. The first thing you see when entering the Royal Room is the big, oval, white floor with curled up borders, like an empty ice rink waiting for its skaters. The shiny snow-white floor reflects the highlights of thousands of silvery twigs, spread across the curved ceiling. Although there are no windows it would appear, through an intelligent lighting-system, that the sun sometimes sends her rays gleaming into the room, followed by the shadows of invisible clouds. During this light experience the air is filled with the crystalline sound of clinking wineglasses, which are hard to recognize having been mounted between the silvery twigs on the sparkling ceiling. Even the specially woven tablecloth seems to mirror the glittery objects above. The inhabitants of the Royal Wing Room are the V.I.P. chairs. All forty-four unique chairs skate across the icy floor with their V.I.P.'s, enjoying their diner-dansant.

Woonbeurs Amsterdam
(Living Fair Amsterdam)

by WATdesign

Client: GOODS
Art Direction/Design: Jan Habraken, Maarten Baptist
Year: 2005

The client had one thing in mind and that was a stand that was affordable and fitted in the companies filosofy (good goods). Inspired on the packaging WATdesign developed the concept to make a fair stand totally out of cardboard. So they designed 3-dimensional wallpaper, giant chandeliers and a floor, out of corrugated cardboard.

The fair stand was purposely built from just 600 dollars of material in 2 hours. Unfortunately the Fire brigade wasn't quite happy with it so they had to impregnate the whole stand (hence the extra 6 hours of building time). And with this simple idea, with the fewest hours and the smallest budget they outperformed the 100.000s dollar stands by winning the best fair stand design.

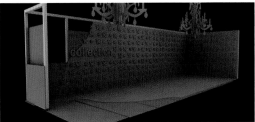

wand constructie vurenhout regels
daarop 3 mm multiplex

plaatsing bouwspots op
regelwerk, aantal ntb

golfkarton op wandconstructie
verlijmen geheel gecertificeerd
impregneren

kroonluchter,
dubbel golfkarton geheel gecertificeerd
impregneren
plaatsing bouwspots op onderzijde

ondervloer 2 lagen 3mm multiplex in
verband gelegd

massief karton 1100 grams geimpregneerd met
magma firestop en aflakken in mat transparant
e.e.a. volvlak verlijmen op ondervloer

plinten uit vurenhout regels 20x55
over gehele hoeklijn

Exhibition Design for
The Churchill Museum
by Nick Bell Design

Client: The Imperial War Museum
Art Direction: Nick Bell
Year: 2003-05

The Churchill Museum, sited in a concrete bunker next to the Cabinet War Rooms in London, is the first ever museum dedicated to the complete life and times of Winston Churchill; an intimate and multifaceted portrait of him, one that reveals the private as well as the public man, his talents as well as his flaws.

The exhibition design for the Churchill Museum comprises 700 separate items of graphics including: 14 non-interactive moving graphic projections, over 20 digital interactive exhibits, nearly 100 minutes of film footage spread across 25 separate film installations, approximately 1500 scanned documents and 500 photographs filed in the Lifeline.

The centrepiece of the Museum is the Lifeline which is essentially a gigantic diary of events spanning Churchill's entire life from his birth in 1874 to his death in 1965. It is an eighteen-metre long interactive table and continuous projection screen served by 13 ceiling mounted data projectors.

Radical or reactionary?

Winston Churchill
'I have mostly ac____
in politics as I f_
wanted to act'

Churchill was always a controversial polit
As a young man, full of optimism,
he was surprisingly radical.

Churchill began his career as a Conservative,
but quickly fell out with his party. In 1904,
he crossed over to the radical Liberal Party.

The Liberals believed something had to be do___
about the widespread poverty and unrest
that existed at that time in Britain.
Over the next ten years,
they introduced many social reforms.

Churchill rose rapidly in the Liberal governmen___
and played a key role in driving through the re___
that laid the foundations of the welfare state___

836

1900

On this day

USA

2 JANUARY 1900

Tokujin Yoshioka × Lexus
L-finesse-Evolving Fiber
Technology

by Tokujin Yoshioka Design

Client: LEXUS
Art Direction/Design: Tokujin Yoshioka
Photography: Nacasa & Partners Inc.
Year: 2006

Part of Milan Design week, the event was taken place at Museo Permanente. Given the interests in fiber technology, the designer has conducted a number of experiments to investigate new possibility for the use of fibers. This has led him to create artifacts that are linked to revolutionary new designs. The abiding potential of fibers has produced the 'PANE chair,' its structure made of nothing but fibers – as if you were sitting on air. Taking the concept of this chair as the starting point, the potential of fiber technology has evolved further since then. When Tokujin Yoshioka teamed up with Lexus and realized that the philosophy of 'L-finesse' shared the same direction as his, he conceived an installation that would fill the very space with fibers, in order to express that idea.

Tokujin Yoshioka views 'L-finesse' as a kind of aura that transcends the bounds of language. 'L-finesse' created a big impression on people by composing whole spaces with fibers that appear just like shapeless particles. The designer hopes people had an opportunity to feel this impression with their whole bodies.

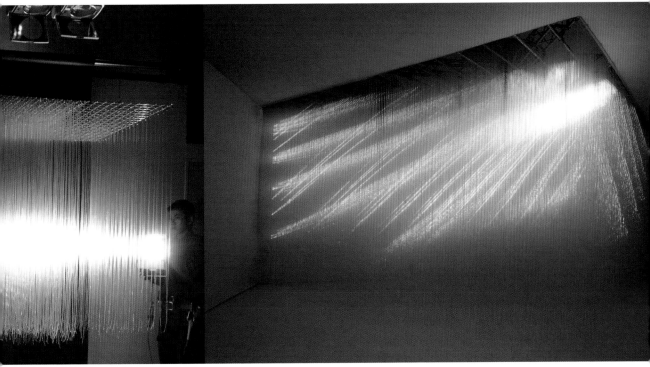

Robot Meme Exhibition

by Tokujin Yoshioka Design

Client: National Museum of Emerging Science and Innovation, Tokyo Japan
Art Direction/Design: Tokujin Yoshioka
Photography: Nacasa & Partners Inc.
Year: 2001

Installation for the Robot Meme Exhibition co-sponsored by National Museum of Emerging Science and Innovation and the International Robot Design Association. Robots born out of the human imagination and the power of science are our future friends, but they are also 'babies' on their way to growing into 'adult humans.' What Tokujin Yoshioka came up with as the ideal for such robots was that of a 'human body,' which is an ultimate design incorporating all kinds of functions. Thus, the designer filled the space with 700 transparent 'bodies' that were created with injected polycarbonate, suggesting a future robot factory. The days when such 'bodies' might turn into our friends could be near.

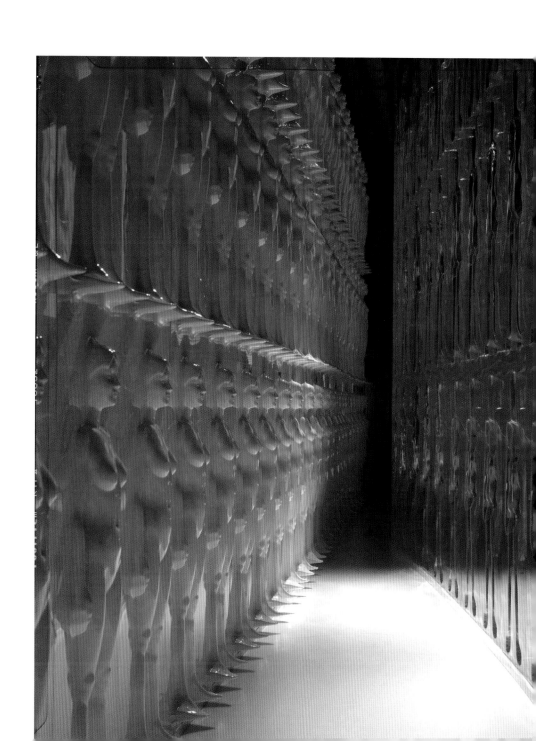

Tokyo Motor Show

by Tokujin Yoshioka Design

Client: TOYOTA
Art Direction/Design: Tokujin Yoshioka
Photography: Nacasa & Partners Inc.
Year: 2005

Tokujin Yoshioka was responsible for the TOYOTA booth design – Reflector Wall (2005).

In order to embody the design philosophy of TOYOTA brand, Tokujin Yoshioka intended to create a TOYOTA booth with a single material under the solid idea.

In designing a booth at the international Tokyo Motor Show 2005, where numerous numbers of cars are displayed, the designer wanted to show off TOYOTA cars with their absolute presence. Then he came to an idea of adopting one of the car components; that was the optical reflector, used for the rear lamp of the car.

More than 100,000 pieces of reflector components are used to cover the entire space. Through its characteristics of reflection and refraction, the reflector brings effects such that even if the space is filled with a number of visitors, you can see distorted multiple images of cars onto the reflector walls.

Tokujin Yoshioka believes that the magical effect of this material has brought the experimental space, where you feel the TOYOTA brand's technology and its appreciation of Japanese aesthetics such like transition and accumulation.

PEUGEOT Metamorphose
by Tokujin Yoshioka Design

Client: PEUGEOT
Art Direction/Design: Tokujin Yoshioka
Year: 2004

In celebration of the national debut of PEUGEOT 307cc, a one-day-event titled 'Metamorphose' was presented at the Spiral Garden. In order to bring out the best of the PEUGEOT brand's automobile design, that is the 'metamorphose' of coupe into cabriolet, Tokujin Yoshioka designed a space where the wind was expressed by the lights.

LED was introduced into the rear lamp of the 307cc model for the very first time. There the designer found the common meaning of design and decided to use LED to cover the whole space.

The space is designed with a huge wraparound LED with netting over 48.6 metres long that emits more than a hundred thousands lights. As if gigantic creature occupies the space, a huge winding LED monitor surrounds the car. A live musical performance by 'sketch show' links to the images and creates a dynamic space by the movement of the LED lights.

Experimental sounds produced by 'sketch show' and images created by the LED lights have the best synergetic effects on creating a completely new design proposal for the motor presentation for PEUGEOT.

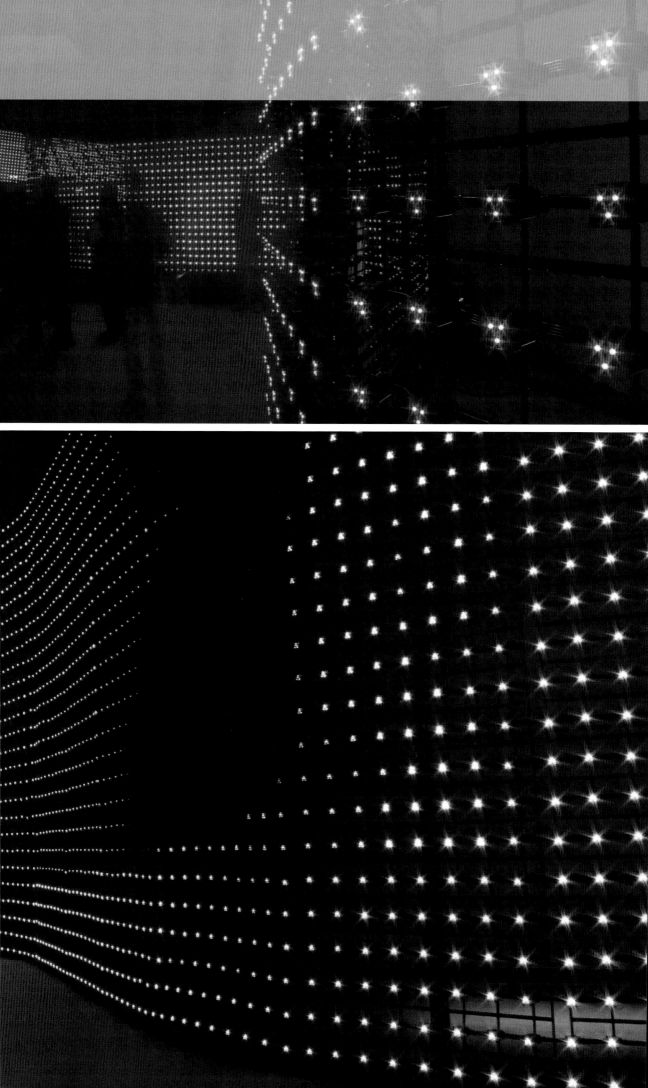

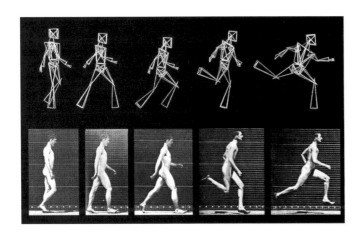

When special effects animators think of high-end computer rendering, Intel is sometimes not even on the list. However a growing percentage of work is being done on that platform. The problem became how to separate out Intel's visuals from the visuals screaming out from their competitors. A second component of the problem was to overcome the stodgy, conservative Intel exhibits used in past years. Fun became a marketing objective.

To attract animators from across the hall, two rows of 20' high 'Polygon People' raced up each side of the exhibit. Consisting of 5 males and 5 females, each 102 polygon runner represents the simplest form of human animated movement on a computer. Each sequence progresses from standing to jogging to sprinting, empha-

sizing the speed of the Intel platform for rendering.

The sisal flooring and cork wall tiles are both renewable resources from sisal plants and cork trees. Most of the exhibit utilized rental walls which walls will be reused hundreds of times. The polygon people are plasma cut recycled aluminum and mostly hollow. They were powder coated to eliminate airborne hydrochemical emissions.

E3 2005 - PSP
by Mauk Design

Client: Playstation - Sony Computer
Entertainment America Inc.
Design: Mitchell Mauk
Year: 2005

E3 stands for Electronic Entertainment Expo. The exhibit was designed to introduce PSP handheld gaming device, PS3 next generation gaming platform, and display depth of games for existing Playstation 2 platform.

This 200' x 200' exhibit attracted tremendous crowds – people waited up to two hours in a line that extended nearly 800 feet.

The PlayStation 3 introduction starts with a dramatic walk along a 160'-long, 15'-high LED screen – the largest indoor screen in the world (for three days). Visitors are coaxed onward by illuminated railings. The wall is a fabric curtain with LED lights sewn in. The result is washes of colour, pattern and motion.

At the curtain, visitors enter a pulsing portal into a waiting area with a warm-up video. When the crowd reaches the theater, they are immersed in the capabilities of PS3 via ultra high-resolution video. Patterns on the walls that glow in the UV lighting lend a space-like depth to the theater. The images are oversized reproductions of the patterns etched on a DVD by a new BluRay laser painted onto two layers of translucent fabric. As visitors emerge from the theater, they encounter the Holy Grail – a shrine-like display of the PS3 unit rotating within a shrine-like cylindrical enclosure.

The uncluttered, pristine rectilinear design of the double-deck PSP Pavilion creates a unique exhibit within

the exhibit. White beamed architecture (styled after 1950's hillside architecture), an illuminated floor and overhead cloud graphics combine to create a serenity that contrasts with the high-energy atmosphere of the rest of the exhibit. The soft, neutral palette provides the perfect backdrop to emphasize the black PSP units and to showcase the dramatic colours produced on their ultra-bright screens. Within the Pavilion visitors encounter rows of spherical transparent hanging chairs. These unique sound-blocking demo stations enable each attendee to have an intimate personal experience with PSP. At the same time, other attendees are able to watch.

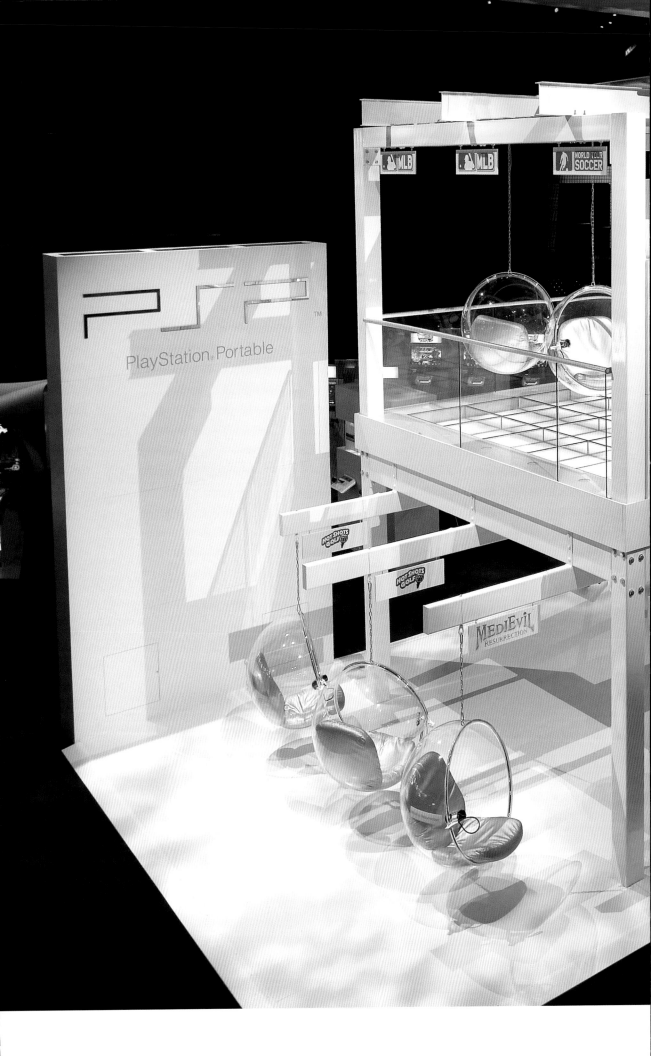

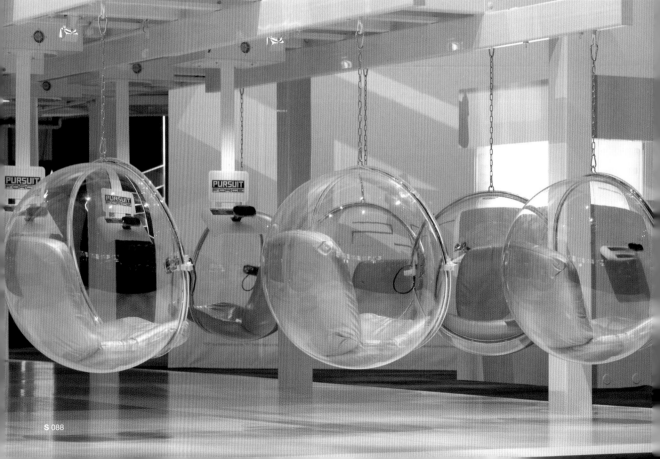

E3 2005 - Xbox

by Purepartner by design, LLC

Client: Microsoft, Xbox 360
Art Direction: Ron Caruso, Chris Pollard
Design: Kinnaresh Mistry
Photography: Jamie Padgett
Year: 2005

E3 stands for Electronic Entertainment Expo. In 2005, as Microsoft prepared to introduce Xbox 360, the company's next-generation gaming console, it identified E3 as the best venue for the launch and secured 35,000 square feet to showcase its new product at the Los Angeles Convention Center.

Purepartner helped Microsoft boost the launch of Xbox 360 by creating an unprecedented on-site gaming experience to communicate the company's core messages. In line with Xbox 360 brand values and identity, the experience was mapped and designed to engage and galvanize the growing gaming community around the Xbox 360 brand. The booth celebrates the vigorous exchange of ideas and a passion for the gaming experience.

Client: PUMA
Art Direction/Design: Marcel Wanders
Year: 2006

Boston, Massachusetts, September 25, 2006 - World renowned Dutch designer Marcel Wanders and the global athletic brand PUMA announced an exciting collaboration at Design Boston 2006. Wanders collaborated with Puma to create a design focused accessories collection for Spring 2007. The collection was unveiled during the Tokyo Design Week on October 31, 2006 and then in New York and Amsterdam in November. The collection is now available globally in all PUMA Stores.

'I love to find new areas for my creativity and create greater value for a larger audience. PUMA has a strong connection to changing culture and wants to stay close to cultural trends by being a leader at the same time. Although we are very different, we both believe we can create added value by inspiring our public in a seductive and creative way.' Marcel Wanders.

'The objective of Puma's co-op projects is for an outside designer to share a different perspective so that we can learn from one another. Marcel Wanders is a pioneer of the unexpected and the ideal partner for us in this venture. PUMA uses collaboration as two worlds coming together to make a product that is unique and fresh.' Antonio Bertone, Director of Global Brand Management for PUMA.

Wanders and PUMA shared the same idea 'I Hate Camping.' The designer explained that he would love to hang out in nature with his friends, however they are urban people. Their rural friends love to go camping, but they can't stand it. They love nature only when the sun shines and the wind has a nice, gentle breeze. In that sense, their love for nature is conditional. With this collection, the designer created items with sophisticated convenience - atmosphere products that help connect people to nature while maintaining an urban, sophisticated air.

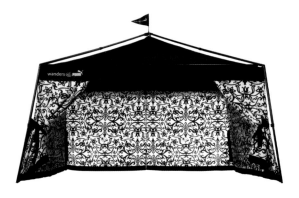

Hong Kong Wetland Park

by MET Studio Design

Client: HK ArchSD (Hong Kong Government's Architectural Services Dept.)
Art Direction: Alex McCuaig
Design: Alex McCuaig, Chris Cawte, Chris White, Lloyd Hicks,
Neil Williams, James Norton, Peter Karn, PK Yu, Sanne van Haastert
Year: 2006

The Hong Kong Wetlands Park and visitor center is the world's largest wetlands eco-park. The new destination venue is set within 145 acres of natural and landscaped wetlands, located on one of the most important avian migration routes in Asia, alongside Hong Kong's Deep Bay. At its heart, semi-submerged below ground level at the approach side beneath a grass canopy roof, is a glass-fronted 90,000 square feet Visitor Centre, designed by ArchSD (the Government's Architectural Services Department) and home to a dynamic range of galleries and attractions, all of which were designed by MET Studio Design, including a real peat swamp featuring live crocodiles. The HK$518m millennial Hong Kong Wetlands Park is Hong Kong's first ever dedicated environmental attraction and is set to become one of Hong Kong's most important tourist destinations, as well as a significant contributor to the Hong Kong economy.

招潮蟹
FIDDLER CRAB

雄蟹擁有大小不一的鉗，不時揮動大螯以吸
引異性的目光，或驅趕其他螯警離開自己的
洞穴。

Male fiddler crabs have one claw that is much
bigger than the other. They wave this claw to
signal to a mate, and to warn other males to
stay away from their burrow.

This page: Human Culture in Hong Kong Wetlands Park

Next page: Wetland Challenge in Hong Kong Wetlands Park

Underground Adventure

by MET Studio Design

Client: The Field Museum Chicago
Art Direction: Alex McCuaig
Design: Alex McCuaig, Ned Phillips,
Pat O'Leary, Helen Lyon
Year: 1999

For one of the America's oldest and most prestigious museums, MET Studio Design was the first ever outside consultancy commissioned for a project of this scope and value - the museum's largest undertaking in a decade.

The designers were briefed to transform an unpromising space - a former basement workshop area with low ceilings and an adjacent entrance/exit - into a robust and permanent exhibition on the subject of soil for audiences of 8 to 80 years old.

By showing the incredible diversity of life in the soil and the importance of our connections to it, the exhibition had to offer a totally immersive, dynamic, entertaining and accessible experience from the most profoundly unglamorous of subjects.

Bloom
by Tronic Studio

Client: Sharp
Art direction/Design: Tronic Studio
Year: 2005

Bloom is a multi-media exhibition by Tronic Studio, for the launch of the HD line of plasma screens called The Aquos by Sharp Electronics in NYC. For their installation, Tronic Studio chose to react on the role of technology in our lives today. After many years where human beings saw technological innovations as a way to dominate nature, a shift in our approach arose. We now understand the fragility of our planet, and focus instead on integrating technology with our environment.

The initial conceptual and visual reference that came to Tronic Studio's mind is that of Art Nouveau, a first attempt to integrate nature and organic shapes into art and architecture dating from the late 19th century. Art Nouveau was characterized by writhing plant forms and was already driven by a desire to integrate natural shapes with design innovations. There was a tension implicit throughout the movement between the decorative and the modern, which can be seen in the work of designers and architects of that time.

Bloom is a multi-media sculptural intervention mixing the latest technologies in CNC milling with the AQUOS LCD televisions. This sculpture depicts the merger of two flows, one red and organic, another one silver and synthetic. As Jesse Seppi, creative director at Tronic Studio puts it: 'I see the piece as a symbol of our position in the world as we relate to technology as a sort of mimicry of nature. We are always trying to play GOD and it has been proven that the human mind does not think like a computer. In fact our minds use quantum theory, which is far less linear than a computer chip, the mainstay of technology. My theory is that if we were ever to mimic nature and all of its complexity we would find ourselves standing in front of the creator. Sharp is pushing to achieve greatness, by way of organic need and synthetic practice, and it is this culmination that drives technology.'

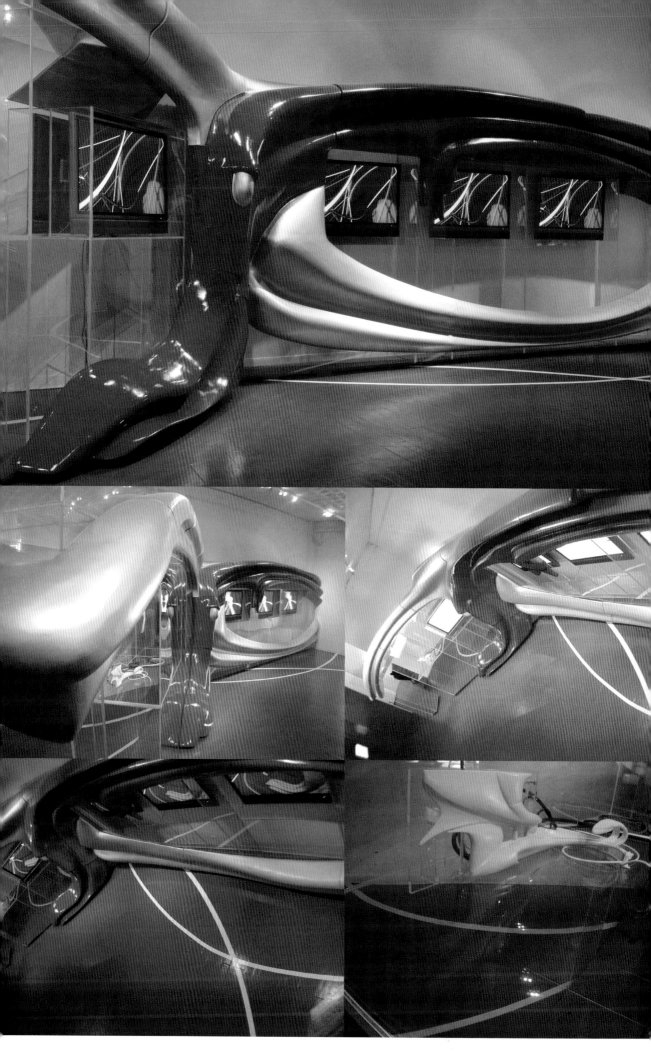

WHEN
ART
MEETS
SPACE

*Spatial, Structural and Graphic Design
for Event and Exhibition*

CONTE|

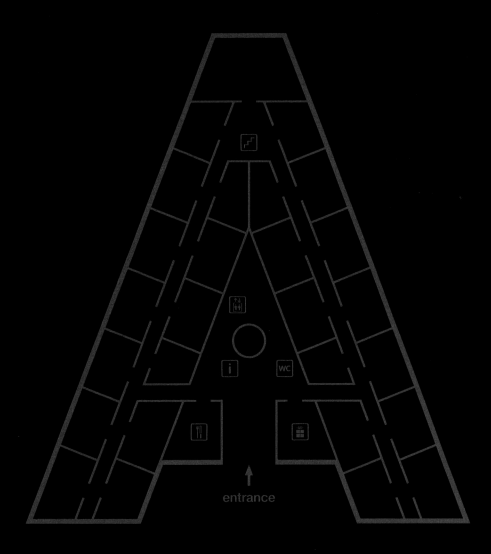

entrance

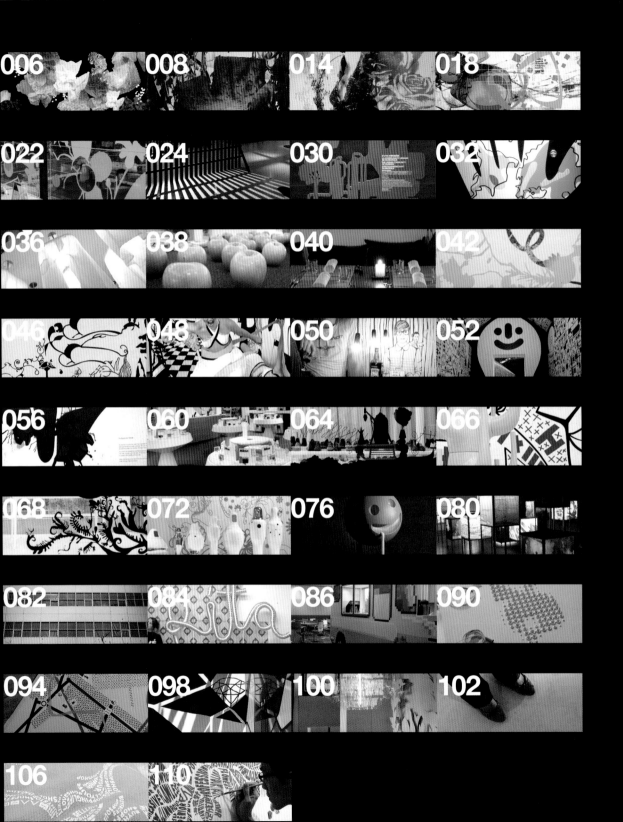

INTRO

Event designers are always the storytellers who actualize abstract concept to tangible event design through accurate assimilation of art like graphic elements in prints, audio and physical installation, with space such as spatial settings and interior decoration. Designing an event is always the creation of a spanking new horizon for you to contemplate and experience.

Event design is a communication process of finding proper form and accurate expression for whatever the content will be, be it through encoding messages to audiences, and controlling the message decoded from audiences with combination of various graphical elements and spatial arrangement. We always try to say something through events, and visitors perceive the messages in their own way.

Not only reading from storybooks, event designers tell you the story by collectively putting all kinds of art in spaces. From captivating settings, exciting audio effects, hot exhibited objects and anything related, designers tell you the story before you step into the event venue. Through the integration of internal factors such as installation, interior decoration, mechanical and computer interactive, audio and performers, and external factors like promotional flyers, posters, invitations and advertising, designers actualize intangible ideas to realistic experiences, and we perceive the messages behind through the entire event experiences. Yet the appearance of the event settings has to be 'meaningful' and 'fascinating' from our viewpoint so as to continue the experience. Imagine if the actors are out of earshot in a drama, if they fail to draw us in, we will never be able to participate neither to contemplate. Same in an event, different fields of design act together in a set. Designers have to impress not only the first row, but also the entire population through spatial and graphic collision in contemplation of event.

However, the decision of whether we attend the events or not is usually made in the very first minute when we come across the news that telling us the events are going to be launched. It is the critic that makes the event breathes or not. Will you go to an event if its posters and invitation cards are dull? Will you spend your day in an exhibition if you cannot even get what it is going to be about from its promotional flyers and advertisement? You don't, right? But i am sure you will love to have a look at the 110% Vujj™ exhibition designed by assistant Co., Ltd and PMKFA if you encounter their promotional items. Have you ever been to the summerhouse of the imaginary spirit king 'European Totoro?' You will be astonished of what it is going to be there if you have an invitation

from 110% Vujj™ in hand, or come across the signage or graphical work produced by the designers. Successful events require excellent graphical elements to be the magnet. No one knows how brilliant the event is if nobody is there.

After you are amazed by the graphics of the promotional items, you will be there in the event, where all kinds of art smash together in the same space to create a brand new nations. You don't stick with commercials and promotional items repeating same graphics and slogans everyday even though you considered them charming at the very beginning, do you? You would rather spend your time in the humorous journeys of events, putting yourself in events with fascinating stage setup which gives you inspiring ideas that you have ever had. Everyone can never forget The End where Artencnica brought fantasy to reality; left all and sundry a 'happily ever after' ending. What is more, Pandarosa has created various incredible works on interaction of art and space. His streamlined and layered graphics with different landscape and natural elements always extend from the origin to the entire space of the venue. The designer uses different materials to produce a delicate and textural image in the Kitchen & Bar of FOX hotel. You will be amazed by Pandarosa's work even you dine at the corner as the graphics are extended to the entire atmosphere of the Kitchen. Are you curious in how Pandarosa's inspiring artwork is produced? Let's come to the showcase where the designer presents the process of artwork in front of your eyes. Flourishing storytellers grab everybody's attention with attractive communication manners, and alter our intrinsic value by impressing us with innovative ideas that we have never come across.

'When Art Meets Space' demonstrates graphical elements designed and developed for any kinds of events. Venue decorations, backdrop design and promotional items such as identity, posters and invitations will be covered. These essentials not only make consistency to reflect the idea of the whole event concept, but also affect the affiliation from the exhibited subjects to audience. You will discover the glamour of graphic elements designed and developed for different kinds of events in this section. Maxalot, Tsang kin-wah, Rinzen and many more will bring you to the wonderland of spatial graphics all over the world. It is a total different world out of daily life that you can never imagine. Let's see how powerful are these work would have blown up your impression for particular events by spreading the pages of this book!

Cenere GB
by Stiletto NYC

Client: Vittorio Cenere
Art Direction/Design: Stiletto NYC
Year: 2006

In 2006, Stiletto NYC designed a store identity for Vittorio Cenere, a high-end fashion store in Italy.

The centre piece of this design was a carpet that inspires all other elements (website, invite) of the store. Each year the carpet is changing and with it the whole look and feel of the store. This time Stiletto NYC came up with the theme 'beautiful trash.' The studio used colourful tissue paper that seems to have been left behind on the black carpet. They were playing with challenging the store and yet keeping with a very elegant idea. The carpet informed the website and Stiletto NYC also extended their design onto store wallpaper.

The End

by Artecnica

Title: The End
Client: Murray Moss
Design: Tord Boontje
Year: 2005

The final exploration of a trilogy based on the designer's exploration of the myths inherent in universal fairy tales. Following the happily ever after concept, The End is like the ending of any popular fairy tale, leaves people with a sense of satisfaction. According to the designer, 'The End is a culmination of ideas that started as prototype. Working with inspired manufacturers enables me to create these pieces that have exactly the same spirit as the original studio-made prototypes. Often we have been able to make improvements by applying new technologies and traditional skills. We have made fantasy becomes reality. The dramatic presentation of The End emphasizes me the emotions locked into the pieces as well as it being a demonstration and celebration of being alive.'

Advertising Posters of Hong Kong in the 1920s & 1930s

by Tommy Li Design Workshop Limited

Client: Hong Kong Heritage Museum
Art Direction: Thomas Siu
Design: Katie Lam, Rika Wong, Kim Hung
Year: 2007

Tommy Li Design Workshop was appointed by The Hong Kong Heritage Museum to design and produce a series of four highlighted exhibitions 'Collections of the Hong Kong Heritage Museum' at the ARTtube of the MTR Central Station in the year 2007. It aims to promote the museum and to arouse people's interest in Hong Kong's heritage by bringing art and culture into our daily lives.

The environment is designed and decorated like window display for shopping owing to the constrain of no entry into the exhibition room at venue. It is a casual and street culture like window show not for product but a variety of cultural stuffs in Hong Kong, which creates a strong visual impact in two layers and combines in one to form 3D effect. The design is a kind of decorative installation which tries to make surprise for passengers, pedestrians across the venue since there is no such full-scale environmental design over the venue before (usually print advertising or notice only). The designers aim to make an impressive experience for even only a 5-minute journey.

Café Bar
by Lief Design

Client: Queen Mary University of London
Design: Martin Vicker
Photography: Mark Enstone
Year: 2005

Lief Design's role was to produce an interior concept to punctuate the architectural creation of Alsop Architects, a new school of Dentistry and Medicine for Queen Mary University of London. The space itself is long and narrow, affording masses of light and a feel of an open gallery. The backdrop of closely pitched orange panels carries through the entire space and creates a rhythm that is visible from the façade, unifying the educational and recreational aspects of the building. The key interior features within the Nucleus are the boldly framed seating booth, the long 'goalpost' dining benches and the contemporary furniture. The seating booth encloses a thirteen-metre long artwork commissioned specifically for the project that was created by 'Kingdom of Ludd,' based in Sydney, Australia. In essence Nucleus represents the notion that interior design should engage with and compliment great architecture.

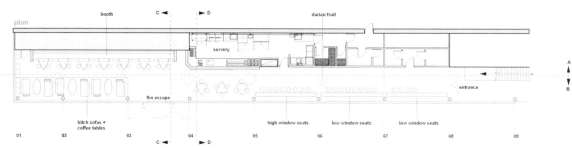

plan

booth   C ◄   ► D   durian fruit

servery

fire escape   entrance

hitch sofas +
coffee tables   high window seats   low window seats   low window seats

01   02   03   C ◄ ► D   05   06   07   08   09

SPACE Furniture
by Pandarosa

Client: : SPACE Furniture
Art Direction/Design: Pandarosa
Photography: Ollie Winter
Year: 2006

The installation was created to launch the new Spring collection of outdoor furniture range. The Space project is a very large (20m W x 4m H) window installation Pandarosa did for SPACE furniture showroom. Florally inspired, the installation was based on a vibrant colour scheme, evoking a sense of warmth and bright fields of colour. Visually it consisted of abstract floral petals, insect creatures and various organic shapes thus creating a garden of imagination and fantasy. The installation was created using a large quantity of vinyl signage.

110% Vujj™

by assistant Co., Ltd, PMKFA

Client: Vujj™
Art Direction/Design: assistant Co., Ltd, Megumi Matsubara, Hiroi Ariyama (exhibition design), PMKFA (graphic design/signage)
Year: 2006

The project is for the launch of the new furniture company Vujj™. The concept theme of the space is 'European Totoro House.' Totoro is an imaginary spirit king that resides in a deep forest in the countryside of Japan. The idea of this exhibition is to create a summer house structured by invisible forest spirits. The exhibition space captures the very moment of an old Swedish summer house turning into forest spirits, the real nature of powerful and humourous fantasy. The house is split into elements and each element becomes a framed stage for a furniture product to be exhibited. All housing elements were care-fully painted into theatre matt black and the lighting cast distorted shadows, extending the exhibition space outwards. The furniture shined up as the only real objects in the whole fantastical space.

Materials: Wood, Polyurethane, Expanded Polystyrene
Dimension of the space/venue: 360m^2
Carpented by: Mitch and Rocky (Shape, London)
Lighting by: Jem White an Louise

This spread: Invitation, signage and graphic work were art-directed by PMKFA. Using the same 'language' of shapes as the assistant's exhibition design to match both the visual identity for Vujj™ and the style of the exhibition to create a teaser of what the visitor would get to see.

Vujj are a young Swedish company dedicated to producing fine quality designs for the international market. Well versed in, but unshackled by, the traditions of Scandinavian design, they seek to add a little provocation to the story.

Vujj takes inspiration from a wide range of sources and there is a strong desire to create works that sit at ease in all environments. Whether it is by referencing the subcultures of our time, what we see in nature, or even the slightly ethereal, Vujj seeks to deliver design that is intuitive, efficient and beautiful.

Every story has a beginning, this is ours.

110% VUJJ. LONDON 2006/09/21-24. PRESS RELEASE.

Address:
Mäster Nilsgatan 1
211 26 Malmö, Sweden
Tel/fax
+46 (0)40 97 27 60
+46 (0)40 97 22 60
E-mail:
info@vujj.com
www.vujj.com

New Scandinavian manufacturer Vujj are proud to present their inaugural range of furniture in the heart of London's Soho at the event 110% Vujj.

On show at 110% Vujj will be designs from Artur Moustafa, Jon Johannes Herbertsson, Karl-Henrik Rennstam and Penny.

A comprehensive collection of furniture is being chairs, easy chairs, tables, chaise longue

Vujj is a young company d
international market
traditions of s
story

World's Fair, in Aichi, Japan. French Pavillion

by Base

Client: Ubifrance, commissariat général de l'exposition Aichi 2005
Art Direction/Design: Base
Year: 2005

Complete identity for the French Pavilion at the 2005 World's Fair in Aichi, Japan, with the theme of sustainable development. The main idea of this work was 'Everything is in everything.' Communications materials, catalogs, and signage were all clear, positive, and comprehensible in any language.

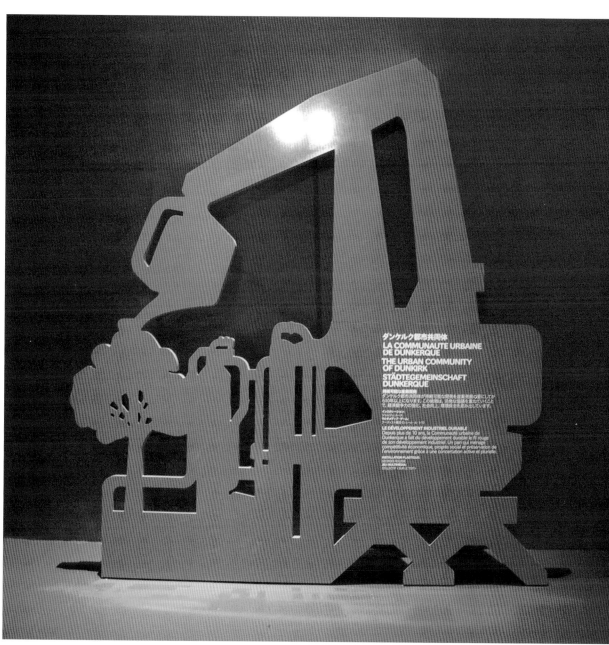

ルイ・ヴィトン
LOUIS VUITTON

自然と共生する製品

環境保護に関する責任を強く感じているルイ・ヴィトンは、自社において温室効果ガス排出量の測定（ADEME（フランス環境・エネルギー管理庁）が開発したメソッド、炭素収支法により計算される温室効果ガスの総量を算出するもの）を導入しました。この調査結果を通じ、ルイ・ヴィトンは会社全体にとって、自社の活動が環境に及ぼす影響を減らすために、自社の優先事項を定めることができるので

出典─インスティチューション資料

CRÉATIF PAR NATURE

La prise de conscience de la Maison Louis Vuitton concernant la protection de l'environnement l'a amené à dresser un Bilan Carbone (méthode mise en place par l'ADEME qui permet de quantifier l'ensemble des émissions de gaz à effet de serre qui résultent d'une activité) au sein même de ses ateliers. Cette démarche lui a permis de fixer les priorités pour réduire l'impact de ses activités sur l'environnement, en mobilisant toute l'entreprise.

CONCEPTION ET RÉALISATION DE L'INSTALLATION
GÉRARD CHALOIN
RÉALISATION AUDIOVISUELLE I.L.L
FILMS D'ENTREPRISE

Camper For Hands.
Communication Design

by Estudio Mariscal

Client: Camper
Art Dirction/Design: Estudio Mariscal
Year: 2006

In the case of the sub-brand Camper for Hands, it means the opening of a new business area for Camper. A company that for 30 years has made shoes now decides to make handbags and to experiment with this line, before anywhere else, in the Japanese market. All these circumstances have inspired Estudio Mariscal in the concept and later development of the logotype and graphic image of Camper for Hands.

The brand, Camper; the place, Japan, and the product, handbags, are the starting points for the logotype of the sub-brand Camper for Hands. The typography arises from the very name 'For Hands' that brings the idea of 'Hand Made.' The writing of the logotype presents a rhythm that is very different to the typographic logotype of Camper, which transmits the idea, of an adult and sensible brand, while the vibrant rhythm of For Hands could be seen as expressing an idea of youth and a new challenge for the company. In spite of this difference, the Camper for Hands logotype is linked with the main brand in order to communicate that the sub-brand is capable of inheriting the same values that make Camper a consolidated firm. For the image Camper created a minimalist concept, starting from the most primitive code of the Camper brand: Red, white and black colours. Keeping in mind the Japanese market, the designer makes a little cultural statement about Japan-Occident, and for this Camper invents a new language whose written form is based on ideograms, the Japanese Kanjis, that graphically represent an idea and are read vertically from top to bottom.

Using Milton Glaser's famous 'I love NY' as a reference point, Camper starts to build, through the use of Kangis and ideograms, the phrase 'Camper loves bags,' and for this the designer draws a foot to symbolize the 'Camper' graphic form, a heart for 'loves' and a hand for 'bags.' From this phrase Camper develops an ideogramatic language that forms phrases that, in reality, don't mean anything but as it happens when one contemplates a painting, everyone tries to interpret it.

In this way, The Camper for Hands graphics is filled with hands, legs, hearts and of objects that are precious or essential to carry in a handbag, on a foot or in the heart. This is the idea that enlightens the language for Camper for Hands, trying at the same time, to never lose the Camper spirit: 'Walk, don't run.'

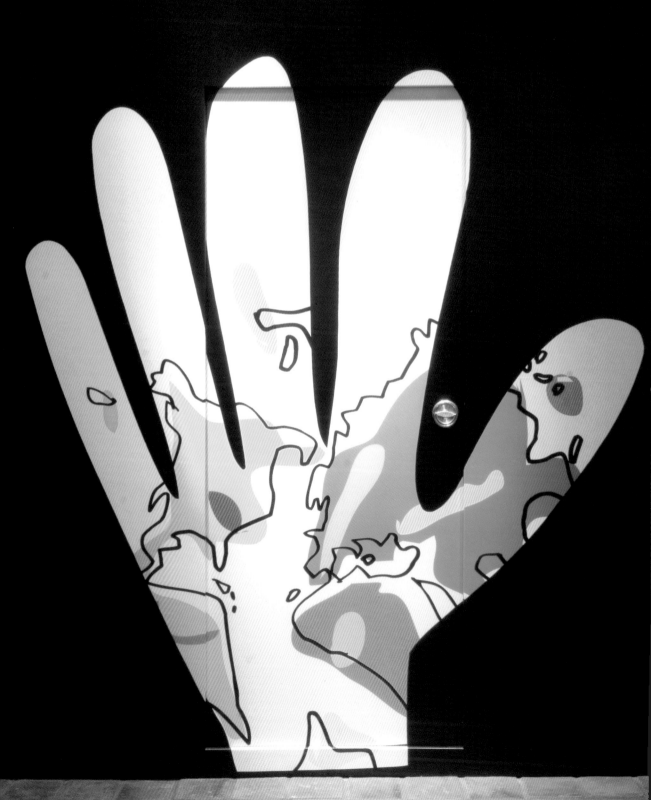

Camper Together with Alfredo Häberli

by Camper

Design: Alfredo Häberli
Photography: Christophe Madamour
Year: 2006

The Together concept had been born in Camper. It now takes on more strength in the new projects that will be presented in limited edition, like this one that has been developed 'together' with Alfredo Häberli.

'Camper is situated on one of the Balearic Islands, in the middle of Europe. For this, in my opinion, the company takes on a totally different status. I love the quality, the sincerity, the fun and creativity of their products. Also their communication. With this support behind me, my contribution to the project of the new store in Paris has consisted in finding simple elements or ideas that, apart from offering a high level image, can also resolve the day to day functions of a shoe store. I placed an island-table in the centre of the space that is large and high, made up of other smaller islands or stones. Their forms and different materials help to organize the shoe families. Lamps in the shape of dresses, trousers, bermudas o shorts hang from the ceiling. They fly above the shoes as if they were the ghost of a human being. They provide warmth and a subtle touch of humour. A curtain runs along one side from the door to the back of this narrow but large space where the cashier is located. On the opposite wall, almost 80 drawings reflect with few lines and nearly no words, the theme of shoes. They are thoughts that have been drawn around this first store for Camper.' Alfredo Häberli.

MusaBook

by MusaWorkLab, Creative Direction
and Design

Client: MusaCollective, IdN (International designers Network)
Art Dirction/Design: Raquel Viana, Paulo Lima,
Ricardo Alexandre
Year: 2006

It is a graphic design collective promotion book. 'Musa' is the Portuguese word to 'Muse,' the source of an artist's inspiration.

During 2003 Musa asked Portuguese designers to submit their work for the edition of the first Portuguese graphic design book with new emergent talents and their work.

From the beginning the designers desired to publish an Inspirational and documental book. A kind of legacy to future designers and promotion of collective work between artists, designers, illustrators, and photographers. Under the concept of a web-based collective they received hundreds of submissions and then made a selection based in quality, originality, technical skills and vision of emerging tendencies. MusaBook was officially presented after 2 years of

the beginning of the project, published by one of the biggest publishing houses in graphic and experimental design – IdN, Hong Kong.

MusaBook presentation was part of the Circuit program, an event occurred in Lisbon 27th to 29th April that Musa was invited to enter. By the subject TASTE defined by Circuit, Musa presented the concept 'EAT GRAPHICS.' Inspired in this concept have been some surprises, making the plugging to MusaBook. Green was the colour of the launching. Hope green. Hope was the word of order of this book, that presented as the 1st compilation book of artists, designers and Portuguese illustrators.

P&A
by Pandarosa

Client: BOX arts space
Art Direction/Design: Pandarosa
Year: 2006

The installation piece, entitled 'P&A' featured a range of decorative paper panels, cutout vinyl highlights, and life-size 3D structure texts drawings of Pandarosa, within a 1.5 m by 1.5 m window front.

The installation aimed to create a portrait of Pandarosa immersed in their own creative wonderland.

Materials: Cardboard, A0 B&W Photocopies, Vinyl, Wallpaper & Texta
Dimensions: Various

FOX Kitchen & Bar

by Pandarosa

Client: FOX kitchen & bar
Art Direction/Design: Pandarosa
Year: 2005

This project is to create graphics decoration for the interior of FOX kitchen & bar at Hotel Fox. It involved a multi-medium approach and was quite collage in nature.

Pandarosa used a diverse range of materials within a single image in order to make the overall feel more delicate and textural. The designers cut out different shapes out of vinyl and wallpaper and layered them together with other shapes and elements related to the kitchen such as utensils and produce. The aesthetic nature of the graphics aimed to express the process of food making from raw produce to presentation.

Materials: Vinyl, Wallpaper, Acrylic paint and ink
Dimensions: Various

Gorgeous
by Pandarosa

Client: Gorgeous
Art Direction/Design: Pandarosa
Year: 2005

It was a fashion driven industry event showcasing various elements within the field including hair, make up, fashion and lifestyle. The piece was created 'live' during the course of the day. The idea was to give people a chance to see the process of the artwork. The image is homage to the work of Audrey Beardsley.

Materials: Wallpaper, Vinyl, A0 Photocopies, Plywood, Paper
Dimensions: 2.4 m x 2.4 m

Channel 5: Make Me A Supermodel

by Container

Client: Channel 5, Tiger Aspect Productions
Art Direction/Design: Container
Year: 2006

This event was part of a reality TV show, in which various potential models competed for a contract with top model agency Select. As part of the show they had to undergo a variety of challenges. One of the tasks they had to face was working with artists – i.e. Container. Container was given free reign by the production company to do whatever the designers wanted to with the group of young hopefuls.

Container's idea was to create an oversized sketchbook – with the models acting as characters from designers' drawing trying to escape. The models wore paper clothes that Container designed and produced, and are 'tearing' out of the book. In addition Container produced some 3D typography, masks and paperbirds. Black ribbon attached to the drawings and continued the black lines from the drawing.

A Haunted House

by Container

Client: Gallery Oel-Früh, Hamburg, Germany, Self Initiated
Art Dirction/Design: Container, Simon Husslein
Year: 2006

Container was invited to create an exhibition/installation at Gallery Oel-Früh, a 60's 3-storey town house in Hamburg.

Container chooses to alter ego's 'the evil twins' to be the focal characters in this project, leading visitors from installation to installation in life size imagery. Visitors enter the show through the basement – being led down a corridor flanked by curtains to the first room, equally enclosed by curtains, illuminated by candles and one of Husslein's light installation. On the ground floor a maze makes visitors drop to their knees to explore the shifting dimensions in the parlor, pantry and drawing room. The attic invites visitors to play hide and seek at the stroke of midnight – with only a torch light to guide visitors and explore all the far flung destinations the 'evil twins' have visited in their travels, until they find another little door, which leads them to a world of optical illusions and eccentric nightmares.

HAPPY LIVING
by Akinori Oishi

Client: PPGroup
Design: Akinori Oishi
Year: 2007

Graphic artwork developed inside the
house at the exhibition HAPPY LIVING in
the MUSEUM of TOMORROW, Taipei Tai-
wan - It's a universe of black and white.
Drawings were all over the space and it can
be imagined as the harmony of colours.
There are small living characters named
'Le Petit Bonhomme' inside the house.
Their smiles could take you to a 'HAPPY
LIVING.'

Perfect Match

by Alexander Turvey,
Ariel Hofstad of Elefant Art

Client: Prior 2 Lever
Art Direciton: Elefant
Design: Alexander Turvey, Ariel Hofstadd
Year: 2006

P2L commissioned Elefant to assist them in creating a visual aesthetic/identity that would help encapsulate the creative freedom of the bespoke P2L brand. This was then brought across to the P2L launch exhibition in April 2006 where the designers allowed their illustration work to bring the launch of Greg Levers first football boot, 'Assassin' to life, whilst making sure to remove the clichéd imagery brought by main stream football associated brands.

Elefant created a brand aesthetic, which demonstrated the freedom of creativity in the P2L shoe launch. The artwork Elefant produced for the P2L identity and launch exhibition is heavily based around the concept of breaking boundaries, for such an inspired product the designers had to creat an inspiring and progressive imagery to match the quality of P2L. Elefant also saw it highly important to utilize the be-spoke aesthetic of the brand, considering the service being offered is of the highest standard. The designers were offered a large range of printing techniques to work with, such as the application of Elefant's prints directly onto leather cow hides.

Due to Prior 2 Lever's most recent development in their novel approach to 3D surface design, Elefant has been the first to demonstrate the versatility of this process, with their graphic illustrative surface decoration, which is applied to the soul of P2Ls bespoke football boot, 'Assassin' designed by Greg Lever-O'Keefe.

The overall impact of the exhibition resulted in a highly tactile experience, allowing Elefant to utilize a vast collection of media, throughout the making process of the boot, and as a highly unconventional canvas for their graphic illustration.

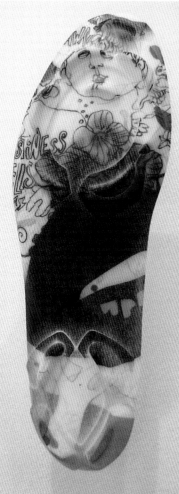

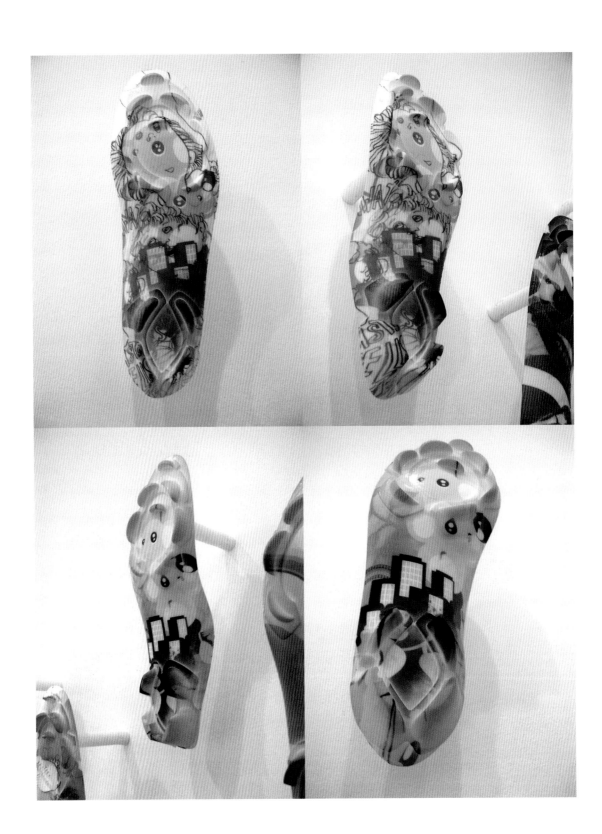

JR Duty Free

by Pandarosa

Client: JR Duty Free
Art Direction/Design: Pandarosa
Year: 2005

To create a group of continuous graphics, which could be incorporated throughout different fixtures, including walls and light dome structures, within all JR duty free retail stores – Pandarosa's visuals aimed to evoke past and capture future fun moments and experiences related to travel, by combining existing travel and cultural images together with various skyscrapes and cloud formations. The aim was to take the viewer away to another world by stimulating their imagination by way of fragmented memory and imaginative expectation. This approach created a more atmospheric, rather than retail-like, experience and visually stimulated thoughts of past and future adventures.

These worlds also induced and excited the viewer into a place of possible individual travel experience.

This spread: Pandarosa's graphics combine existing travel and cultural images together with various skyscrapes and cloud formations so as to evoke and capture fun moments and experiences related to travel.

Camper Together with Jaime Hayon

by Camper

Client: Camper
Design: Jaime Hayon from HAYON®STUDIO
Year: 2006

The Together concept was already born in Camper but had not yet been written. It now takes on even more strength in the new projects, that will be in limited edition, like this one that has been created 'together' with Jaime Hayon. Adding the experience of one to the wit and charm of the other, the Majorcan Company follows the line of diversity versus the repetition that has been established in the world of commercial interior design. Camper continues innovating and in favour of new languages that communicate the essence of the brand while always maintaining loyal to its original spirit.

Jaime Hayon returns again to the British capital to project the Camper store in Foubert's Place. He has conceived it as an installation in which the concept shop-gallery is developed. There are few creators that like him have the capacity to fuse together, in ones own particular style, the frontiers that normally separate the worlds of art and design. And so, the new store is a personal interpretation of the Camper universe seen through Hayon's imagination. The best of his repertoire is condensed in this work. His characteristic drawings, the fantasy of porcelain and exclusive hand crafted furnishings: They are all here.

The manual work and the appreciation for things well made, produced with quality so that they last, as it was long ago, but without undervaluing modern technologies, is one of the identity signs of this artist from Madrid. The lamps that were designed exclusively for Camper, for example, are born from the Majorcan tradition of terracotta, a millenary material that in this case was treated with a spray in order to join it to the brilliant Venetian porcelain in a unique and sophisticated cooking process. It is the traditional and the modern that also walk 'together' in the new culture of contemporary design.

Camper and Jaime Hayon cordially invites you to attend
the inauguration of a new vision in the world of retail design.
Please join us for a cocktail and experience
the **Camper Together** concept with us at.

5-7 Fouberts Place
London W1F7PY
On September 21, 2006
6.00 - 9.00 pm

RSVP Ruth Coughlan
Communications Manager Camper UK
Tlf +44 207 409 3114
Email rcoughlan@camper.com

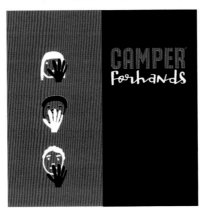

Camper cordially invites you
to the reopening of
Camper Omotesando
With the presence of
Javier Mariscal from
Mariscal design Studio.
You will visualize the
transformation of the
Omotesando shop
in person and
enjoy cocktail following.

Place Camper Omotesando Tokyo
Date 13th of September. 2006
from 6pm～

Lorenzo fluxa

マリスカル・デザイン・スタジオの
ハビエル・マリスカル氏をお招きし
改装を
行うことになりました。
マリスカル氏がデザインし
新しく生まれ変わったショップを
ご覧頂きながら
カクテルを楽しんでいただきたい
存じます。

場所 :カンペール表参道
日時 : 2006 年 9 月 13 日（水
午後 6 時～

Mediterranean Digital Baroque Installation

by HAYON®STUDIO

Client: David Gill Galeries
Art Direction/Design: Jaime Hayon
Photography: Nienke Klunder
Year: 2003

The project was presented for the first time in autumn 2003 at David Gill Galleries in London.

Featured creatures that sign and defend the root of creation, a Bisazza covered house with an army of toys living inside, supersonic pig seatings, handmade wall graphics engulfed in a metamorphic fragile traditional ceramic forest.

This installation was a vital and ironic manifesto about Hayon's personal cosmogony that is devised of mature languages from heterogenic worlds: his birthplace, Madrid, the francophone culture from his childhood and his skateboarding adolescence.

AQHayon at the Design Museum, London

by HAYON®STUDIO

Client: Artquitect Editions
Art Direction: Ramon Ubeda
Design: Jaime Hayon
Photography: Nienke Klunder
Year: 2004

The Design Museum presented Jaime Hayon's AQHayon Collection in their exterior tank as a selection of a breakthrough design piece.

The Installation, that included the bathroom collection and graphic applications, was exhibited during summer 2005.

Mon Cirque
by HAYON®STUDIO

Client/Art Direction/Design: Jaime Hayon
Photography: Nienke Klunder
Year: 2005

The circus is a great, lost world of intense characters and distant frontiers. A remote place of the past and tradition almost lost. Perhaps a great inspiration, a source of shapes, liveliness, melancholy and colour, the Mon Cirque installation is the designer's vision of a large metaphor. A place that symbolizes his hope of artistic freedom, where the designer's work is free to transcend the frontiers built between design and art. The classical colourfulness of the circus is replaced by a more serious and elegant contrast between black, white and gold: Cirque de lux. Vases become characters, clowns become lamps, plates used as canvas, tables grow legs. A sophisticated ambient where craftsmanship is a key element. Avoiding the use of molds, a return to the hand made object where each piece is unique in its existence, like the characters they represent. Mon Cirque was presented in Barcelona in 2005 and traveled to Minneapolis, Lisbon, Paris and Cologne.

In the Milky Night

Year: 2006

by Rinzen

'In The Milky Night' is the inaugural issue of Rinzen's planned series of 'Care Packs' – concentrated doses of visual nourishment to be opened and read in times of aesthetic crisis.

To celebrate the launch of the Care Pack, Rinzen held simultaneous exhibitions in Berlin and Sydney – exhibiting work from the book, as well as specially created works and installations.

In keeping with the theme of the Care Pack, Rinzen transformed the expansive Neurotitan Gallery in Berlin into the depths of space – as a backdrop for a series of paintings on wood and canvas, pieces in watercolour and ink, large-scale photographs, sculptural elements and installations and projections.

Revolving galaxies (courtesy of the Rinzen designed gobo for Mathmos' Space Projector) overlapped walls of tiled posters, and glowing red eyes peered out of a hidden cupboard. A wall scrawled with distorted red 'Rinzen' typography sat behind a large blue drooling head, and Rinzen's bike for Japanese company Bebike was suspended from the ceiling. The Sydney show at the Monster Children Gallery featured an installation of a series of gigantic foam heads and hands melting into the floor. A large hand shot 'sparks' of lighting across the ceiling, against the background of geometric red and blue Rinzen posters.

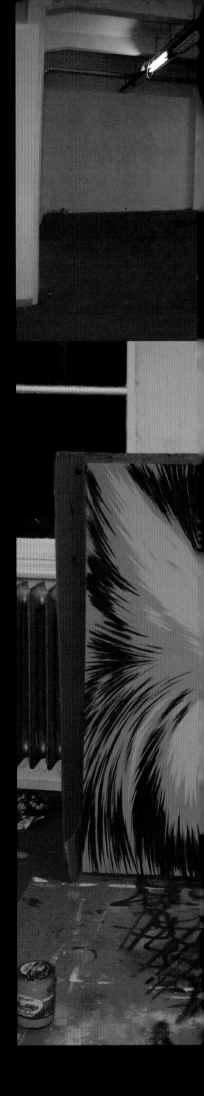

To Be A Poet Is To See
– Ibsen In Our Time

by Motorfinger

*Client: Sixsides, Ministry of foreign affairs, Folkemuseet
Art Direction/Design: Motorfinger graphic design and
illustration, Sixsides – exhibition designer
Year: 2006*

An exhibition highlighting the universal themes of Henrik Ibsen's work. The exhibition is currently touring the world. It highlights the universal themes Ibsen explored in his dramas, which are still politically relevant today: political power, idealism, globalization, gender equality, corruption, individual freedom, child neglect, freedom of speech and environmental protection, etc.

The concept was to illustrate Ibsen's tekst. For example, one of the cubes was based on the theater play 'Peer Gynt' and the contemporary tekst was about globalization. Designers combined these two by making the cube illustrated with Peer's attributes and the challenges of the globalization.

The cubes were made of aluminum rack with printed canvas wrapped around. There were three different canvases: see-through, semi see-through and glossy latex. All the cubes had Mdf wood figures inside which were part of the story to the cubes. The cubes were lit from inside. The corruption cube was lit with red light.

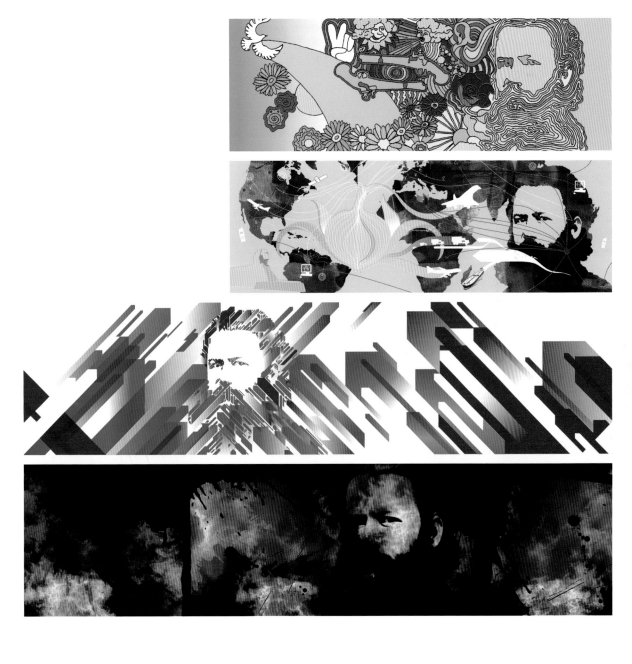

Todays Art Festival 2006, The Hague

by Maxalot

Client: Todays Art (The Generator)
Art Direction: Max Akkerman
Design: eBoy, WeWorkForThem, Build, Inocuo, Kenzo Minami, Pixelnouveau, Universal Everything, Marco Eschler,
Peter Zuiderwijk, Maxalot
Photography: Maxalot team
Year: 2006

In the centre of The Hague, the stylish white city hall by architect Richard Meier functioned as a public space gallery when 10 of the worlds finest graphic designers and illustrators, used the big white surfaces of the structure as their canvas. Through hi-end projection equipment, two installations that incorporated some of the world's strongest slide projectors, the building was lit up by artworks especially created for this show that were designed to fit the elements of the building to change the city's central square into an exhibition space for the two nights of the festival. The installation was responsible for a slide-show as big as 32 x 32 metres. Visitors to the festival enjoyed seeing the building's change facade every 15 minutes, making each design show 4 times over two days. For each design, one image was created using 4 powerful 7000W Hardware Xenon DHX slide projectors with Reichman 220 MM lens installed by ADCPRO from Belgium, each carrying one 18 x 18cm slide, projecting from two sides of the building.

DesignMade 2006 Exhibition the Manifesto of Annual Design 2006 - On Line

by The Hangaram Design Museum

Art Direction: In Kee Chang (Curator)
Design: The Hangaram Design Museum
Year: 2006

'Design MADE 2006' is held as a secondary exhibition following its first show in 2005. Design MADE literally means to realize images, try and make through the medium of materials for certain purpose. However, in the other hand, 'MADE' is abbreviated from 'Manifesto for Annual Design Exhibition,' which stands for dual meaning of announcing a start of a new exhibition. Design MADE is the exhibition searching the design which produces the value of our lives and pleasure beyond making visionary aesthetics.

Designers got together here out of their routine lives. Their stories about 'line' in our daily lives endlessly continue. It can be a line or it can be a string, or it can also be a silhouette that is shaped by a line.

Line is everywhere. But the exhibition is about the infinite possibility that a line can create. It's about reinterpreting the lines in an ordinary object and discovering the potential. The exhibition consists of three sections: 'Enjoy Line' with fun imagination, 'Extension Line' which experiments on diverse changes by combining new materials, and 'Secret Line' where designers try to communicate with audience in an extremely controlled manner. From the exhibition room to the rest rooms, nothing was untouched by the designers. In its effort to provide energy to your daily life out of the boring routine, 'Design MADE' brings all kinds of artists together to declare the new, bold and edgy design.

DesignMade 2006 Exhibition the Manifesto of Annual Design 2006 - On Line

Interior design office
ILSE media
by WATdesign

Client: ILSEmedia
Art Direction/Design: Jan Habraken, Maarten Baptist
Year: 2005

How to create a flexible office for 10 companies in 1 space with a lousy budget? WATdesign created a shipload of giant props, all made out of 2D graphic elements. As the companies with one graphic thing in common, the pixel, the environment is designed as one giant Sim-city office garden. A UK post-van is the mailing box. An Ice-cream van is the office buffet, telephone poles harboring the cables etc. etc. Together with transparent stickers every product was stuck to have the same look all-over.

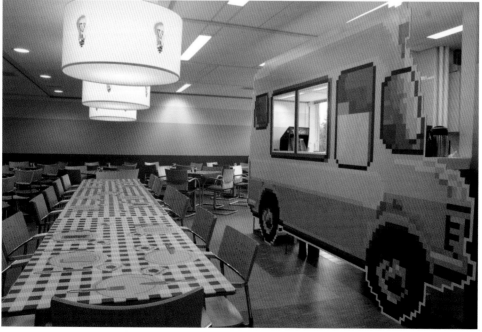

A 088

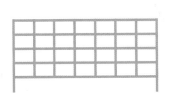

2x plaat op U profielen lijmen

1x onderplaat

On/Off [& Everything In Between]

by Build, Commonwealth, Maxalot

Art Direction: Max Akkerman (Maxalot), Lotje Sodderland (Maxalot)
Design: Michael C. Place (Build), Zoe Coombes (Commonwealth),
Francisco David Boira (Commonwealth)
Photography: Grupo On/Off - Maxalot, Commonwealth, Build,
Timothy Saccenti
Year: 2006

ON/OFF was the first of an ongoing collaborative series, Commonwealth vs. It was the launch event of Brooklyn's Espeis Archetype Gallery which opened in June 2006.

The central works were a creative merge between graphic works by Michael C. Place, and print-specific frames, designed by Commonwealth. The frames were traced with a continuation of the graphics, together making them, and the prints they housed, a perfectly merged artwork. The frames were produced using sheets of Arctic White Corian in Commonwealth's Digital Production Laboratory that is purposefully visible from the Espeis Gallery. The finished frames measure 92 x 112 cm.

The On/Off Show incorporated 10 print-in-frame sets, giant banners, vinyl graphics on glass, and a giant overhead projection running in the corner of the gallery. There were also promotional postcards which were handed out prior to the event. Event posters and tee shirts which were sold on the night, and online afterwards. The opening night music was hosted by NYC Photographer and DJ Timothy Saccenti on decks.

The Commonwealth vs. is an invitational series that brings together the brutality of architecture, and the insane precision found in the digital arts. By working freely across disciplines, these collaborative works use industrial modes of digital prototyping as a means of creating authentically-digital, material objects.

2morrows kingdom cargo

by Pandarosa

Client: Melbourne festival
Art Direction: Pandarosa
Design: Pandarosa, Kongzilla & AKA ltd
Year: 2006

The project aims to create an analogue interactive space by creating a 'blank landscape' which viewers could interact and categorize as they wished. All around the world, today's kingdoms are divided into zones, suburbs and states. These 'divisions' are encountered by all of us on a daily basis, yet we never question their existence.

What if we had a 'blank landscape' kingdom which we could categorize in any way we wished? What kind of 'divisions' would we make? By creating this 'blank landscape' Pandarosa asks, 'Can there be a kingdom without divisions? Can this create equality? Are divisions necessary to create social status and hierarchy? Will you create a divided or unified kingdom?' These outcomes rely on our own participation.

Here's how you can make your choices – Pick up your 'KEY TO KINGDOM' card and select from the various 'icons' and 'patterns' available to you. Once selected stick them onto the 'blank landscape,' you can position as many or as few as you wish amongst the others, to create your place in society. The icons are assigned with meanings but feel free to reassign them to suit you.

Materials: Stickers, Core flute, Electrical tape, Audio scape & scissors
Dimensions: Various

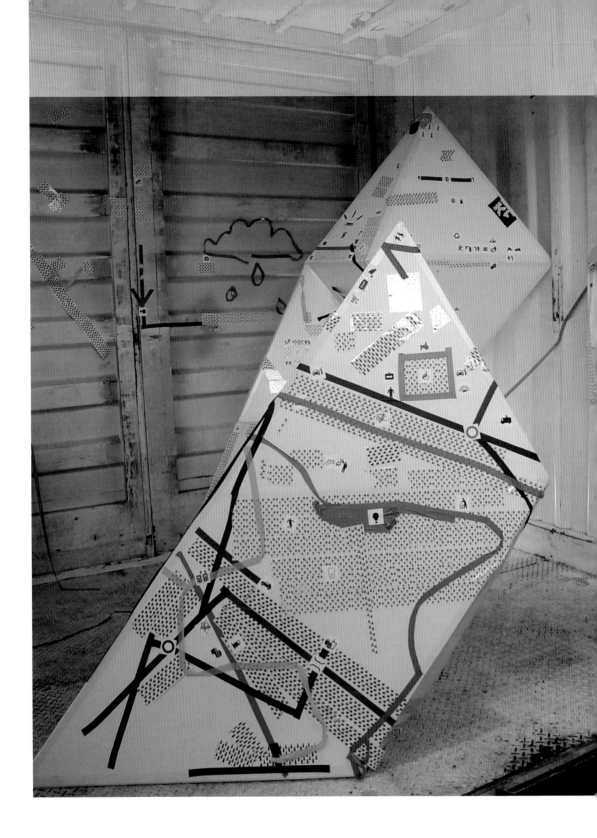

TRANSLATION Group Show
by Pandarosa

Client: Gallery 101
Art Direction/Design: Pandarosa
Year: 2005

It is a group exhibition that investigates the distorted and multifaceted elements of translation in visual art.

'Shadows in a diamond cave' was a painting that stretched beyond the wall and onto a nearby window. The incorporation of the gallery space made the piece physically dominating and blurred the sense of 'inside' and 'outside' by turning the gallery itself into part of the work. By engaging both the gallery and other works in the exhibit Pandarosa wished to invite the viewer to explore the possibilities of collaboration between artist and with space.

Materials: Vinyl, Acrylic paint, Ink, Silk screens
Dimensions: Various

Bienale, st Etienne (France), Designfair Kortrijk (Belgium)

by WATdesign

Client: Design connection Eindhoven
Art Direction: Jan Habraken, Maarten Baptist
Design: Frieke Severs
Year: 2005

This project is to design a fairs stand made out of the packaging from the exhibition products for only 17,000 dollars, which can be reused, and rebuild in different settings. As with WATdesign previous positive relationship with cardboard products, they proposed to build a fairs stand out of cardboard boxes. The boxes can be used for transportation as well as for building the fair stand. They designed a closed box that can be opened by perforations to create a display. Together with the closed boxes they can create walls. To spice up things they designed some pop-up theme walls, which can be fold up for transportation and be re-used. By using a portable ink-jet writer the designers can make the additional text on every box. Simple and clever.

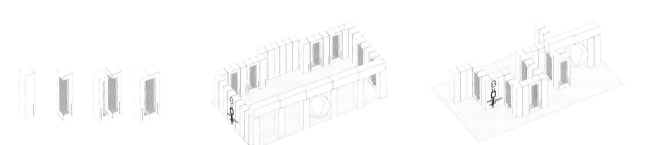

In the Dark, in the Darkness

by Tsang Kin-wah

Art Direction/Design: Tsang Kin-wah
Year: 2006

This is Tsang's solo exhibition at a gallery called 'Art-U room' in Tokyo where he used the gallery space to make the installation work.

The dimensions are 3.75 x 4.45 m with materials of cold transparent lamination film and light projection. The statement is 'He spoke and cut men in two... After the division the two parts of man, each desiring his other half, came together, and threw their arms about one another, entwined in mutual embraces, longing to grow into one; they were on the point of dying from hunger and self-neglect...' The designer's inspiration is 'Where are you and... when can I meet you again...'

MEGartSTORE

by Tsang Kin-wah

Client: Hong Kong Heritage Museum
Art Direction/Design: Tsang Kin-wah
Year: 2006

'When it comes to a serious shopping experience, Hong Kong has everything in abundance.' As the Hong Kong Tourism Board slogan suggests, Hong Kong has long enjoyed a reputation as a shopper's paradise. Now, if you are looking for access to art that is as easy as shopping in a shopping mall, 'MEGartSTORE' is your handy solution.

Putting the spotlight on over 300 museum art collections, the 'MEGartSTORE' is the first big-box store of its kind in Hong Kong. Five artists – Tang Ying-chi, Annie Wan, Hung Lam, Amy Cheung and Tsang Kin-wah – showcase their works in five shops. The interior of the 'MEGartSTORE' has been specially designed by four young architects, Steven Chu, Anson Tsang, Kenneth Tse and Humphrey Wong, with branding by Tommy Li.

Debuting in Hong Kong with the aim of examining the dialogue between museum exhibition and commercial presentation, 'MEGartSTORE' provides an alternative 'consumption' experience for shoppers and spectators alike, while also serving as a catalyst for a new perspective on our everyday shopping behaviour.

The statement is 'I shop. You shop. Everyone shop. Everyone goes shopping and everywhere is shopping. Everyone tells you to shop. Media such as TV, newspaper, radio, screen, etc. is everywhere and everywhere is advertisement. Even when you are in the toilet, you can still find their existence. They induce you to shop and ask you to buy. We are all living in a shopping environment. Shopping has become the basic instinct and the living behaviour of everyone.'

EXIT

A 110

Permanent Installation – Shu Uemura

by Tsang Kin-wah

Client: Shu Uemura, Luxury Products Division of L'oreal USA, Inc.
Art Direction/Design: Tsang Kin-wah
Year: 2006

This is a commission project that carried for Shu Uemura, USA for their new boutique in Costa Mesa, California where they invited Tsang to make a permanent installation work at the boutique based on the background and history of Shu Uemura.

The work is mainly based on the difference and uniqueness of the backgrounds of the boutique, its founder, Mr. Shu Uemura (Japanese culture), the artist (Chinese culture) and its location (American culture). The juxtaposition of these cultures creates quite an interesting relationship that let people think about how the East and the West meets and views each other. There-

fore, this becomes one of the main themes in choosing and designing the texts and the pattern, a traditional peony and pheonix textile. At the same time, the view on beauty and makeup is also another main theme in making the work and choosing the texts.

Tsang projected the image on the walls and ceiling of the boutique by using an overhead projector and then traced all the texts and image. After that the designer filled all of them in different colours.

WHEN SPACE MEETS ART/
WHEN ART MEETS SPACE

Spatial, Structural and Graphic Design for Event and Exhibition

Published and distributed in Europe by:

Index Book, SL
Consell de Cent, 160 local 3
08015 Barcelona, Spain
Phone: +34 93 454 5547
Fax: +34 93 454 8438
ib@indexbook.com
www.indexbook.com

Published and distributed for the rest of the world by

viction:ary™

viction:workshop ltd.
URL: www.victionary.com
Email: we@victionary.com

Book design by viction:design workshop
Concepts & art direction by Victor Cheung

Acknowledgements

We would like to thank all the designers and companies who
made a significant contribution to the compilation of this book.
Without them this project would not have been possible.

We would also like to thank all the producers for their invaluable
assistance throughout. Its successful completion also owes a
great deal to many professionals in the creative industry who
have given us precious insights and comments. We are also very
grateful to many other people whose names do not appear on the
credits but have made specific input and continuous support the
whole time.

Future Editions

If you would like to contribute to the next edition of Victionary,
please email us your details to submit@victionary.com

TOKUJIN
YOSHIOKA
DESIGN

Born in 1967 and learned design from Shiro Kuramata and Issey Miyake, Yoshioka established Tokujin Yoshioka Design in 2000. His works includes shop design for ISSEY MIYAKE and A-POC, as well as installations for exhibition ISSEY MIYAKE Making Things at Cartier Foundation in Paris, which has gained a high evaluation over the globe. The designer's special design includes HERMES and TOYOTA. Other design includes Honey-pop, Tokyo-pop, ToFu, Media Skin and PANE chair. His works are now found in the permanent collections of the MoMA and other major museums around the world. Yoshioka has always undertaken experimental designs.

Page S068-081

TOMMY LI
DESIGN
WORKSHOP
LIMITED

Tommy Li is Hong Kong's master designer in this generation renowned for his 'Black Humour' and 'Audacious Visual' designs. Spanning Hong Kong, China, Macau and Japan, he is one of few designers to have penetrated the international market.

Over the years, Tommy was received almost 500 awards. His most distinct achievement to date has been record owner to receive 4 awards from New York Directors' Club, which honours outstanding results among Chinese designers.

Page S052-055, A014-017

TRONIC
STUDIO

Tronic is a NYC based multi-media studio founded in 2001 by Columbia Architecture graduates Jesse Seppi and Vivian Rosenthal. Their work moves between film, animation, architecture and experiential design. They have delivered unique digital visions for both RES and Creative Review; directed and animated spots for Nike, Fuse, MTV, HBO and NEC; conceived and executed projects for Diesel, GE, Sharp and Wired (in store), Nike and Visionaire (online). In general, the designers have worked to eliminate lines delineating one form of creative media output from another. These visual futurists are boldly combining architecture, graphic design, film and animation through new uses of technology to create striking and conceptually based work.

Page S110-112

TSANG
KIN-WAH

Graduated from the Chinese University of Hong Kong in 2000, Tsang Kin-wah received his master degree from Camberwell College of Arts, the London Institute in 2003.

Tsang's works mainly focus on investigating the specific meanings created by combining swear words with elegant image and by presenting this as a form of wallpaper. He specifically creates different installation works for different sites and venues. Among these years, Tsang has taken part in various group exhibitions in Europe and Asia, and has his solo exhibitions in various cities like Tokyo, Barcelona, Madrid, etc.

Tsang has received awards likes Tokyo TDC Prize 2007, 2005 Sovereign Asian Art Prize, Prize of Excellence – Hong Kong Art Biennial 2001, etc. His works are collected by Sovereign Art Foundation, Museum of Design Zurich (Switzerland), Shu Uemura (Costa Mesa, California) etc.

Page A102-112

WATDESIGN

WATdesign is a multidisciplinary design firm started by Jan Habraken and Maarten Baptist. Both graduated at the Design Academy Eindhoven where they established themselves in the city of Eindhoven with their newborn studio WATdesign. The name WATdesign stands for Working Apart Together, representing the way of working of the designers. Under leadership of Jan and Maarten, other disciplinary and skilled talents are asked to participate in projects when needed. This successful way of working resulted in an impressive clientele. Other than corporate projects WATdesign also initiates their own designs in order to keep fresh and innovated.

Page S062-063, A086-089, A100-101

NICK BELL DESIGN

Nick Bell Design is an independent, multi-disciplinary graphic design consultancy based in London. Their approach to visual communication is driven by a close attention to context. Nick Bell, their director, was the creative director of Eye, the highly influential international review of graphic design from 1997 to 2005. His experience on Eye enabled him to develop a more curatorial method of editorial design – one his studio has adapted very successfully for the design of exhibitions. Clients included the V&A, the Science Museum, Tate, the British Council, National Portrait Gallery and the new award-winning Churchill Museum in London.

PANDAROSA

Ariel Aguilera & Andrea Benyi are the love children behind Pandarosa, a group which specializes in creating cultural graphics, but has also expanded their visual approach to include outcomes in exhibition, installation, projection, short film, website animation and interior based projects. The pair has received acclaim for their interior decoration work produced for Hotel Fox in Copenhagen, and was recently invited back to produce further work for the hotel's new restaurant 'FOX kitchen.' Pandarosa has created projects for clients such as Adidas, Puma, Lee, JR Duty Free, Fat4 and Euroluce.

Their illustrative work has appeared in many magazines including Soma, Grafik, Tokion, Icon, and Frame, and their multimedia pieces have been showed at various festivals including DOTMOV, ONEDOTZERO, AMODA, CONTRAST and CRACOW FILM FESTIVAL.

PROJECT PROJECTS

Project Projects is a design studio focusing on print, environmental, and interactive work for clients in the cultural sector. Founded in January 2004 by Prem Krishnamurthy and Adam Michaels, the studio's clients include Artists Space, Creative Time, D'Amelio Terras gallery, Independent Curators International, Lower Manhattan Cultural Council, Lyn Rice Architects, Metropolis magazine, The New York Times Magazine, Princeton Architectural Press, Steven Holl Architects, Van Alen Institute, and the Whitney Museum of American Art. Project Projects also collaborates with architects, artists and writers on self-initiated projects.

PUREPARTNER BY DESIGN, LLC

Purepartner by design is a New York City brand marketing and design firm that dimensionalizes the world's leading lifestyle brands.

Purepartner is comprised of marketing-driven design professionals who develop creative solutions to meet marketing objectives. Creating impact, achieving contact and communicating the brand essence in an immersive environment is how Purepartner creates preference and drives business.

RINZEN

Australian design and art collective Rinzen is best known for their collaborative and illustrative approach, creating utopian alternative realities and other worlds.

Rinzen's posters and album covers have been exhibited at the Louvre and their large-scale artwork installed in Tokyo's Zero Gate and Copenhagen's Hotel Fox. They recently designed the inaugural issue of Paul Pope's Batman for DC Comics and graphics for a bicycle released by Japanese company, Bebike.

Members of the five-person group are currently based in Sydney, Brisbane and Berlin.

STILETTO NYC

Stiletto NYC is a design studio based in New York & Milan, that specializes in art direction & design for print and video. It was co-founded in 2000 by Stefanie Barth and Julie Hirschfeld. Stiletto works with such clients as MTV, Nike, CondeNast, HBO, HKM films, architect Andrea Tognon, the New York fashion collective Threeasfour and several boutiques & individuals in Europe and America. Stiletto has been featured in publications internationally and spoke at Semi-permanent design conference in Sydney Australia in 2006.

THE HANGARAM DESIGN MUSEUM

The Hangaram Design Museum opened as a public museum and has been managed by the Ministry of Culture and Tourism of Korea. Since its opening in 1999, the Hangaram Design Museum has held various design exhibitions such as 'Bruno Munari (2002),' 'Archigram (2003),' 'Droog (2003),' 'From Body to Universe-European New Way(s) of Life (2002)' from Centre Pompidou in Paris, 'Jonathan Barnbrook (2004)' and 'László Moholy-Nagy (2005).' These exhibitions served the purpose of introducing International Design trends and the famous designers to Korean public.

MATHIEU LEHANNEUR

Mathieu Lehanneur graduated from the ENSCI-Les Ateliers (Ecole Nationale Superieure de creation industrielle) in 2001. His graduation project is a Galenic design proposal addressing the question of how to design medications from the perspective of the patient/illness relationship. The same year, he was awarded an ANVAR research grant.

In 2001 he established his own studio and works on product design and exhibition design projects. He received the Carte Blanche VIA in 2006 and he was awarded the Grand Prix de la Création, Paris. Since 2004, he is Post-graduate research Manager at Cité du Design/Ecole des Beaux-Arts de St Etienne. He is part of the permanent collection of MoMA, New York, MoMA, San Francisco, FRAC, Paris.

Page S028-029

MAUK DESIGN

Mitchell Mauk is the Principal of Mauk Design, which he founded in San Francisco in 1986. Mauk Design specializes in exhibit design and corporate communications, and puts special emphasis on the marketing integration of two- and three-dimensional images. Mitchell Mauk has won multiple gold and silver awards from the IDSA, SEGD and other competitions, and was named Exhibit Designer of the Year by Exhibitor Magazine.

Mauk was the first American designer to have a light design manufactured by the prestigious Italian lighting firm Artemide. His work has been featured in Communication Arts, Interiors & Sources, VM+SD, AXIS, and Graphis, and is in the Permanent Collection of the Library of Congress. He has appeared on television in interviews for CNN's 'Business Unusual.'

Mauk is a graduate of Art Center College of Design in Pasadena. He began his career at Bass/Yeager Associates, followed by Designworks, the southern California industrial design firm owned by BMW. At Mark Anderson Design in Palo Alto, he was Senior Art Director and was involved in developing the graphic image of the early Apple computers, as well as corporate identity for Duncan Aviation, and Herman Miller's Office Pavilion.

Page S082-091

MAXALOT

Lotje Sodderland and Max Akkerman met at Club Baby in Amsterdam, where Lotje was features editor of the niche magazine readBaby while Max was director of exhibitions and events. With a background in political science, Lotje divides her time between her documentary production company, Elk Creatïf and securing global domination for Maxalot. Max studied multimedia and worked for several years as a graphic designer, but soon he decided to leave the creation to the masters and started exhibiting their work in gallery settings and producing creative events. Combining the unique creative vision with the love of design and spatial aesthetics, Maxalot is the perfect platform to realize his mission in promoting modern digital art.

Page A082-083

MET STUDIO DESIGN

MET Studio Design is a multi-award-winning British exhibition and interior design consultancy, with a long record of highly successful projects in the Far East and South East Asia, as well as in the UK, mainland Europe and the USA. The company won a Queen's Award for Enterprise for its design services overseas in 2004. The company was originally formed in 1982 by Alex McCuaig and since then it has built a formidable international reputation for exciting and intelligent work, with an enviable reputation for creativity, innovation and efficient delivery of ground-breaking visitor experiences worldwide – from corporate venues to museums, exhibitions and zoos.

Page S100-109

META4 DESIGN FORUM LTD

Meta4 Design Forum is an architectural and design firm newly established in 2001, aiming at delivering works which are less explored in the local architectural scene. The idea of setting up the firm was initially materialized after winning the first endorsed architectural competition in Hong Kong. With the flourishing creativity the designers see in foreign architectural works, they believe that such atmosphere for innovative concepts can be brought not only to the profession in Hong Kong, but also to the market in China and other places. The studio space will always be in a state of flux, transforming from a mere work space to a live architectural forum; or from an exhibition venue for art pieces to whatever event one fancies. By all means, architecture should always be a treat.

Page S056-059

MIGLIORE +SERVETTO ARCHITETTI ASSOCIATI

Architects Ico Migliore and Mara Servetto work in the fields of architecture and concept design exhibition. Their projects are characterized by the way in which they define space through the experimental use of light and the construction of dynamic landscapes. Both are Professors of Exhibit Design at the Polytechnic in Milan, where they have worked with Achille Castiglioni since 1989. The designers also hold workshops and lectures in many Italian and international universities. Ico Migliore is Visiting Professor at Kuwazawa Design School in Tokyo. In 2004 they have been invited to participate at the IX Venice Architecture Biennale 'Metamorph' and in 2006 at the exhibition 'Architects' exhibition designs' hosted by Pavillon de L'Arsenal in Paris. In 2006 they have obtained the 'Gold Award' in the 20th 'Annual Exhibit Design Awards.'

Page S006-019

MOTORFINGER

Expect nothing, just imagine.

Page A080-081

MUSAWORKLAB, CREATIVE DIRECTION AND DESIGN

Formed in 2003 by Raquel Viana, Paulo Lima and Ricardo Alexandre, a Lisbon based collective of graphic designers. Musa work with as many aspects of design as possible from artistic/experimental to commercial. The first big event made by the collective was MusaTour2004 supporting MusaBook project, the first Portuguese emergent graphic design book ever compiled, published by idN, Hong Kong. With MusaCollective, local boundaries were broken and projects such as NLFMagazine, the first Portuguese Qee, all the exclusive/limited merchandising and the commercial works developed by MusaWorkLab put the Portuguese design scene on a higher stage of international visibility. At the end of 2005 and earlier 2006 MusaCollective presented out of Portugal MusaTour, promoting new talented designers in Barcelona, Tokyo and published the NLFMagazine book by Singapore publishing house BasheerGraphicBooks. MusaCollective tries to be seriously involved in as many fun projects as they are allowed to.

Page A038-039

CAMPER

In 1981 Camper opened its first store in Barcelona. After commercializing its product for seven years in conventional multi-brand stores, they had come to the realization that their shoes needed a different atmosphere that would allow for interaction with the brand and in which one could enter into their real environment. With this objective Camper developed their own concept for a store: A shoe store that displayed all their styles and sizes. It was completely revolutionary. The stores became a window through which Camper could exhibit its shoes and its philosophy to the world.

At the beginning of the 90's Camper began its international expansion and realized that all stores of all brands in all shopping areas and in all cities, were alike. The character of the city, its culture, was diluted in an interior design that, although carefully projected, eventually became aseptic. For Camper, concepts like identity and diversity always go together, and for this reason the concept of global becoming uniform was not theirs. From this observation came the idea to make each store different, each one with its own personality.

Page A036-037, A064-065

CONTAINER

Container is a multi-disciplinary art and design partnership based in east London. Besides traditional illustration they have explored interior design, fashion, installations, animation and product design. Nicola Carter and Luise Vormittag first met while studying Graphic Design at Camberwell College of Art, London. Container was launched in spring 2003. Since then they have illustrated for numerous books and magazines, made window displays, redesigned a café in Selfridges' department store, created hotel rooms, developed the prize-winning identity for a MTV programme as well as working on a range of non-commercial projects - from participating in exhibition projects to building their own haunted house.

Page A048-051

ESTUDIO MARISCAL

Since Javier Mariscal (Valencia, 1950) took up a pencil in the 1970s to earn his living, his life and his career have been characterized by his creative incontinence, by his need to express himself through multiple disciplines, whether artistic ones or not. Furniture design, painting, sculpture, illustration, interior design, graphic design, landscape painting, gardening, horticulture and so on have been the object of his professional, vital activity. Mariscal expresses himself by means of a personal language that is complex in its intention and simple in its declaration, innocent and provocative at the same time, that serves him to innovate, to risk himself and communicate, to carry on tickling the eyes of those who gaze upon his work and to create complicity with the other person.

Page A032-035

HAYON®STUDIO

Jaime Hayon was born in Madrid, Spain in 1974 and trained as an industrial designer in Madrid and Paris. Began working as a researcher in Fabrica, Italy in 1997, he started his individual career in 2004 and has kept his hands full with eclectic projects. From toys, to furniture and interior design as well as artistic installations, his boldness has been transcending the borders of the often-separated worlds of art and design, merging his own style with ease between the two. Currently with a new base in Barcelona, Hayón has been awarded by Wallpaper as one of the 10 breakthrough creators worldwide as well as the 2006 Elle Deco International Award and the Icon Magazine Best Show award for the 2006 London design week. Jaime's work has been featured in all major design publications and newspapers worldwide.

Page A066-075

KARIM RASHID INC.

Karim Rashid is a leading figure in the fields of product and interior design, fashion, furniture, as well as lighting and art. Born in Cairo, half Egyptian/half English, and raised in Canada, Karim now practices in New York. He is best known for bringing his democratic design sensibility to mass audiences. Working with an impressive array of clients, Karim is radically changing the aesthetics of product design, and the nature of the consumer culture in which we now live. To date, Karim has had some 2000 objects put into production. In addition Karim has successfully entered the realm of architecture and interiors.

Page S048-051

LIEF DESIGN

Lief Design, led by Martin Vicker, is a small consultancy that thrives on a steady flow of challenging design briefs. Clients range from corporate bar/restaurant chains, through to independent retail and nightclub operators. Vicker's enthusiastic approach promotes constant investigation and inspires originality in terms of formal and spatial solutions.

'Interior design is about packaging a business for commercial and operational efficiency' explains Vicker. 'Our aim is to fuse this with concept ideas that relate to the combined vision and ambition of our clients and their customers.'

Page A018-021

MARCEL WANDERS STUDIO

Marcel Wanders' fame started with his iconic Knotted Chair, which he produced for Droog Design in 1996. He is now ubiquitous, designing for the biggest European contemporary design manufacturers like B&B Italia, Bisazza, Poliform, Moroso, Flos, Boffi, Cappellini, Droog Design and Moooi of which he is also the art director and co-owner. Additionally, Marcel Wanders works on architectural and interior design projects and recently turned his attention to consumer home appliances. Various designs of Marcel Wanders have been selected for the most important design collections and exhibitions in the world, like the Museum of Modern Art in New York and San Francisco, the V&A Museum in London, the Stedelijk Museum in Amsterdam, Museum Boijmans van Beuningen in Rotterdam, the Central Museum in Utrecht, Museum of Decorative Arts Copenhagen and various Droog Design exhibitions. Marcel Wanders has recently been elected Elle Decoration's International Designer of the Year. In his studio the designs for the global market are developed. Marcel Wanders studio is divided into product design and interior design teams.

Page S060-061, S096-099

AKINORI OISHI

Born in 1972 Japan. The designer studied fine arts at Kyoto City University of Art, and media-designs at IAMAS (International Academy of Media Arts and Sciences). Since the winning in MILIA (International Multimedia Fair in France) 2001, the designer had worked at the French creative studio TEAMCHMAN from 2001 to 2003. Oishi is now an independent artist, and teaches media-designs at ECAL (Ecole Cantonale d'Art de Lausanne) in Switzerland, and Tama University in Tokyo.

In the year 2001, Oishi's interactive art game 'OPNIYAMA' was exhibited at the opening show of the contemporary museum 'Palais de Tokyo' in Paris. The designer also produced the animation DVD for the Swiss documentary film 'Mais im Bundeshuus' in 2005, and be invited to the world character arts festival 'Pictoplasma Conference' in Berlin in 2006.

Page A052-055

ALEXANDER TURVEY & ARIEL HOFSTAD OF ELEFANT ART

During the first collaborative project of Alexander Turvey and Ariel Hofstat together, the vision of Elefant was first initiated. Throughout the design process the designers realized they had a unique working partnership, and a growing passion to create. Both with aspirations of nurturing their own company, and a strong work ethic, a very small and determined Elefant began to grow.

The year following graduation of Turvey and Hofstat, they worked in design studios, but Elefant became their continued obsession. It was the place there the designers would escape to at night, they thrived on the work they were creating and the freedom the designers had been given. This accelerated Turvey's and Hofstat's use of visual language and style to something quite unique, and the designers were able to design within their own process.

The process by which the designers work forms the distinct character of Elefant. Elefantart, as we are more formally known, conceptually likes to challenge design guidelines, whilst continuing to consciously realize the central role of the client and of the brief.

Page A056-059

ARTECNICA

Artecnica, an internationally known, award-winning design power house with mission to create products that blend art and technology.

As its name describes, the mission of Artecnica is to create products that blend Art and Technology in equal measure where Art represents the aesthetic value or form while Technology represents the utilitarian value or function

Artecnica's products produced by conventional factories and artisan communities, with a commitment to its 'Design with Conscience' campaign.

Artecnica's products are part of MOMA's permanent collection and sold through museum and high end design stores.

Page A008-013

ASSISTANT CO., LTD AND PMKFA

Assistant is a creative group that uses three guiding themes throughout their work. These themes are urbanism & tourism, space & situation and money & consumerism. Assistant founded by Megumi Matsubara, Hiroi Ariyama and Motohiro Sunouchi originally began as an interdisciplinary design practice in 2002. They take an experimental approach to evolve their work and philosophy. Their work spans from space and architectural design to product design, interactive design, and art exhibitions. In 2005, they have formalized themselves as assistant Co., Ltd. – International and Interdisciplinary Design Practice. Ever since the start, free and liberated creation has been developed with assistant, through the collaboration with various artists and clients around the world.

Page A024-029

BASE

Formed in Brussels in 1993, Base is made up of 45 people working from studios in Brussels, New York, Barcelona, Madrid and Paris. The studio specializes in creative direction and brand development. As an addition to its identity work, Base in 2004 launched a writing division, BaseWORDS. In 2005, the studio added two further complementary departments: BaseMOTION, specializing in film and motion graphics, and BaseLAB, which designs custom typefaces and builds design-oriented tools. The agency also invested in Books on the Move, a comprehensive book publisher offering services in design, editorial, printing, and worldwide distribution. With a clientele that spans the corporate, cultural, and institutional sectors, Base has worked on a broad range of projects, from creating image campaigns to designing identities for major corporations and institutions.

Page S020-023, S030-031, A030-031

BROWNS

Established in 1998, Browns is an independent, multi-disciplinary design consultancy based in London. Browns produces intelligent and considered communication solutions for a diverse range of clients over a wide range of disciplines. The approach of the consultancy is a straightforward one, a belief in simplicity, clarity of message and originality in delivery.

Page S036-037

BRUCE MAU DESIGN INC.

With over twenty years experience, Bruce Mau Design (BMD) brings to any project a uniquely experienced, talented and diversely creative team whose knowledge base spans an eclectic range of backgrounds including art, graphic design, architecture, engineering, the sciences, archeology, publishing, filmmaking, business strategy and communications.

In resisting the simple solution in favour of the real opportunities inherent in a project, BMD has gained international recognition for its expertise and innovation across a wide range of projects achieved in collaboration with some of the world's leading architects and institutions, artists and entrepreneurs, writers, curators, academics and businesses.

Bruce Mau Design is part of the MDC Partners network, one of the world's foremost multi-disciplinary communication firms.

Page S038-047

BUILD

Build is a Graphic Design studio which prides itself on its craft-like approach to print. It was founded in 2001 by Michael C. Place & Nicky Place & has since established itself as a studio with an almost obsessive attention to detail. Projects range from one end of the creative spectrum to the other and [almost] everything in between!

Build is Michael, Nicky, Brockmann & Betty.

Build. Print With Love.

Page A090-093

AKINORI OISHI / ALEXANDER TURVEY & ARIEL HOFSTAD OF ELEFANT ART / ARTECNICA / ASSISTANT CO., LTD AND PMKFA / BASE / BROWNS / BRUCE MAU DESIGN INC. / BUILD / CAMPER / CONTAINER / ESTUDIO MARISCAL / HAYON®STUDIO / KARIM RASHID INC. / LIEF DESIGN / MARCEL WANDERS STUDIO / MATHIEU LEHANNEUR / MAUK DESIGN / MAXALOT / MET STUDIO DESIGN / META4 DESIGN FORUM LTD. / MIGLIORE+SERVETTO ARCHITETTI ASSOCIATI / MOTORFINGER / MUSAWORKLAB CREATIVE DIRECTION AND DESIGN / NICK BELL DESIGN / PANDAROSA / PROJECT PROJECTS / PUREPARTNER BY DESIGN, LLC / RINZEN / STILETTO NYC / THE HANGARAM DESIGN MUSEUM / TOKUJIN YOSHIOKA DESIGN / TOMMY LI DESIGN WORKSHOP LIMITED / TRONIC STUDIO / TSANG KIN-WAH / WATDESIGN